Waves of Change

Kyle Butt and Stan Butt Jr.

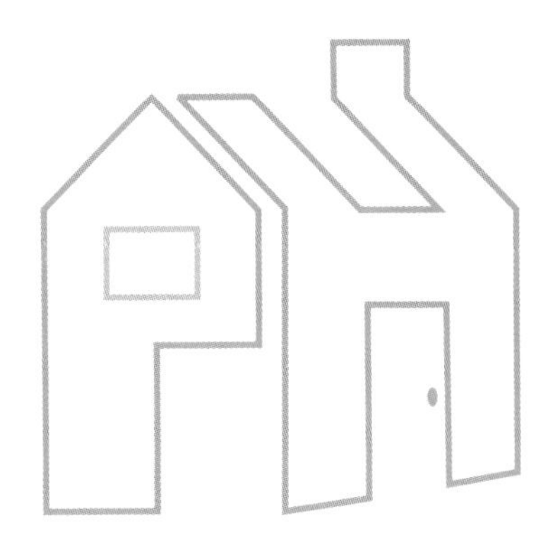

Peaceful House Publishing
3617 N. Georgetown Drive
Montgomery, Alabama

ISBN: 0-9762140-0-8
Printed in China

TABLE OF CONTENTS

FOREWORD

Wave after wave pounded the rocky shoreline.

Mark had never experienced such waves.

He'd read about them. He'd seen pictures. But somehow the articles, pictures, and movies hadn't captured the real power of the waves. The descriptions fell far short of the reality. The spray off the rocks, for one thing—he had never thought about the ocean spray when he looked at the pictures. It was hard to keep his eyes open on the shore because of the constant salt water spraying off the rocks. And the sound. Mark had never felt anything like it. It wasn't just sound that he heard with your ears. It was sound he felt with his whole body. The pounding of the waves seemed to rattle his teeth. His whole body trembled with the power of the sound. His ribs shook. His head ached. His family had tried to talk a little on the beach, but the sound of the crashing waves made it impossible to hear even a shout.

This was everything he had imagined—and much more!

Eight months ago, fifteen-year old Mark had taken up surfing. Since he lived in south Georgia, the trip to the Florida coastline wasn't that long. He'd managed to save up enough for a board from money he made mowing yards. He had already been able to use it several times. Steve, the youth ministry intern and all-around cool guy at Mark's congregation, was an accomplished surfer who was giving Mark lessons. Steve had surfed all over the world–California, Australia, Brazil, and Hawaii. With Steve's help and encouragement, Mark's confidence and ability grew. He was surfing the mild Florida waves easily.

Then two months ago, the family announcement had been made. Mark's dad was going to Hawaii for a two-week business trip, and the whole family was going with him. Mark could hardly believe his luck. He was going to Hawaii. And he was going to surf some *REAL* waves.

So here he was.

Out here alone. Belly down on his board. Scared and shaking. His parents watched nervously from the shore. They hadn't liked the idea. And he could tell from their feeble waves and fake smiles that they still didn't like it. To tell the truth, he wasn't sure he liked it either. But it was too late. Here he was, and it was now or never.

The problem was he didn't know which wave to try. One looked too fast. One looked too big. The next looked too small. He just didn't know. So, he waited...and waited. What would Steve do? Which would he choose? Steve wasn't here to decide for him now. His mom and dad didn't know anything about surfing, and they couldn't help from the shore anyway.

He was really alone for one of the first times in his life. It was up to him. It was his decision to make. It was an important decision and a dangerous one. If he chose wrongly, he might end up seriously injured. But, oh, if he chose the right wave! Think of it! Riding the might of the ocean. The deafening sound. The awesome power. He knew he would never forget it.

So he did all there was to do. He remembered all of Steve's teaching. He remembered everything he'd read and studied about surfing and wave selection. He chose his wave, and he hopped on his board. He chose his wave carefully and. . . .

Mark's story is not unlike your own. You might never have been on a surf board in your life or even been swimming in the ocean. But you have faced, or will face, moments of decision; times when you'll be all alone with a big, important decision to make. Times when you'll have to rely on the teaching and instruction you've received. Times when you'll have to remember what you've read and studied.

For many young people, this time of testing, this moment of decision, comes when they leave home and go to college. Everything is tested. Everything becomes a decision—especially matters of faith. Mom and dad aren't there to wake you up on Sunday morning to make sure you get to Bible class. Your youth minister, preacher, and even your Christian friends aren't around. Choices about faith are now up to you now.

Waves of change are crashing all around us. Many of those waves of change involve the Bible doctrines of the Church that belongs to Christ. False teachers are calling for change. "The world is changing; so should the church," they argue. But what they forget is that the Bible is not changing. The Lord's will for the Church in A.D. 2005 is the same as it was in A.D. 35.

The apostle Paul encouraged the Ephesian Christians to grow in faith and knowledge. Only then would they would be able to handle the waves of change. He taught that if we build up our knowledge in the teachings of Christ

> "...we should no longer be children, tossed to and fro and carried about with every wind of doctrine, by the trickery of men, in the cunning craftiness by which they lie in wait to deceive, but, speaking the truth in love, may grow up in all things into Him who is the head—Christ" (Ephesians 4:14-15).

It is our hope and prayer that you will build the house of your faith on the foundation of Christ and His teachings. Then when waves of error and unscriptural change crash against that foundation, your faith will stand. Only by remembering those things that you have learned from godly Christian teachers, and your own study of the Bible, will you be able to choose wisely among the waves of change that are coming in your time.

Kyle Butt
& Stan Butt Jr.
June 2005

"Then Jesus came and spoke to them, saying, 'All authority has been given to Me in heaven and on earth.' "

Matthew 28:18

If we do everything "in the name of the Lord Jesus," that means we do those things that Christ gives us the permission to do.

CHAPTER 1

WHO HAS THE RIGHT?

You are getting out of your car in the Wal-Mart parking lot when a shiny red convertible pulls into the parking spot next to you. The driver gets out of the car, sees you, and strikes up a conversation. You make a few comments about the nice car, and he mentions that it is for sale. In fact, he tells you that he will give you a great deal on it. The car is for sale for the bargain price of $1,000. Wow! That sounds like a great deal to you so you buy it (I know you don't generally keep that kind of cash in your pocket, but use your imagination).

Cruising down the street in your new, red convertible feels great. You can tell that everyone is watching you, wishing they had a car like yours. As you pull up to a stop light, you notice a police car behind you. Unconcerned because you have not broken any laws, you slowly pull away when the light turns green. The patrol car follows. Finally, his lights start flashing, and he pulls you over. He asks for your license as he looks the car over very carefully. Then he asks you to step out of the car. "Where did you get this car?" asks the policeman. "I just bought it officer," you answer nervously. The officer looks at you and says, "Looks like you just lost your money, friend, because this car is stolen. I am afraid we are going to have to take it to its rightful owner."

But you paid for the car. Why don't you get to keep it?

You don't get to keep the car, because the person who sold it to you did not own it. He did not have the right to sell it. He did not have the authority.

AUTHORITY

Most of us understand the principle of authority quite well. If a man off the street bangs on your door in the middle of the night and demands that you let him in, you call 911. But if a police officer, with a search warrant and a badge, knocks on your door at the same time of night and instructs you to open up "in the name of the law," then you let him in. Why? Because the police officer has been given the authority by the government to come into your house. But the man off the street has not been given that authority.

Think about this example of authority. If your five-year-old brother storms into your room and tells you to get off the phone, you probably pause your phone conversation long enough to tell him to go away, and then keep talking. Yet, if you are talking on the phone to that same friend, and your father knocks on the door, and tells it is time you to get off the phone, that is an entirely different situation (at least it should be, according to Ephesians 6:1).

So who gets to make the rules? Who says that your dad can tell you what to do, but your little brother can't? Who says that you must open the door for the police but not for a strange man off the street? Who has the authority to make the rules?

The very simple answer to that question is Jesus Christ. He has been given **all** authority. He sets the rules. In Matthew 28:18, the Bible says: "And Jesus came and spoke to them, saying, 'All authority has been given to Me in heaven and on earth.' " Jesus told His disciples that He had been given the authority (by God) to make all the rules.

Let's think about that for just a minute. Jesus is not the one who decides how fast the speed limit should be. He is not the one who decides what time you have to come in at night. How does He have all authority? The answer to that is simple. He has delegated some authority to other people. That means that He has given certain people or groups the right to make some rules based on **His** rules.

For instance, Romans 13:1 says: "Let every soul be subject to the governing authorities. For there is no authority except from God, and the authorities that exist are appointed by God." In this verse we learn that God gives governments the authority to make certain rules. Governments have the authority to tax people. They have the authority to set speed limits and many other similar things. Their authority stops, however, when they make a law that goes against something found in God's Word. In Acts 5:29, the apostle Peter and others told the authorities that they would not stop preaching about Jesus because they "ought to obey God rather than men."

In the same way, God has given your parents the right to make rules for you. In Ephesians 6:1-2, we read: "Children, obey your parents in the Lord, for this is right. 'Honor your father and mother,' which is the first commandment with promise." Your parents have been given the authority to decide where you go, what time you must come in and other things like that. Just like the governmental authority, however, parental authority stops if they attempt to make rules that go against the Bible. If parents tell their children they must lie, cheat, or steal, they have overstepped their authority. God has not given them the authority to make rules that go against His Word.

THINKING SPIRITUALLY ABOUT AUTHORITY

Now that we understand authority, we need to apply this principle to spiritual things. Suppose you were in a lunch line and one of your classmates dropped his lunch tray. As he did that, he sinned by saying a curse word. Could you walk over and say to your friend that his sin of cursing is forgiven? Yes, you could say that, but would his sin be forgiven just because you said it? No. Does a teacher or principal have the authority to forgive the student's sin? No again. The only person who has the authority to forgive sins is Jesus.

Mark 2:1-12 tells a very interesting story about four friends of a paralyzed man. Believing that Jesus could heal their friend, the four men tried to get into the house where Jesus was teaching. Unable to get through the door because of the large crowd, the men took their friend onto the roof, removed some of the tile, and lowered him down to see Jesus. They expected Jesus to heal their friend. When Jesus saw their faith, he said to the paralyzed man, "Your sins are forgiven you." The Jewish scribes who heard Jesus were angry. They correctly believed that no one could forgive sins but God. That was Jesus' entire point. He was showing the people that He was God in the flesh. He had the power to forgive sins. In order to further prove that He was God, He healed the paralyzed man. The scribes were right to believe that only God has the authority to forgive sins. They were wrong not to recognize that Jesus was God in the flesh, Who had the authority to heal and to forgive sins.

Today it is the same. God has given Jesus the authority to forgive sins. If we obey the words of Jesus and the inspired Bible writers, to whom Jesus gave authority, we will be forgiven of our sins. If we do not obey Jesus, then we cannot be forgiven. No preacher, parent, or teacher on Earth today has the authority to create a different way to be saved, than what the Bible says. Only God's Word, the Bible, has the authority to tell us what we must do. For instance, we should not lie. Why not? Should we tell the truth because others will like us better? Should we tell the truth because it always feels better? Not really. We should not lie because the inspired Bible writers tell us not to lie, and the Bible has the authority to tell us how to live. [As a side note, please remember that every one of the rules that God makes is for our own good. God created us and knows exactly how we ought to live in order to be happy. Just like a parent knows that a child needs to eat vegetables and cannot survive on chocolate cake all his life, God knows what our spiritual needs are.]

WORSHIP & AUTHORITY

What about worship? Let's apply this principle of authority. First, we must remember that God makes the rules in worship. He is the only one who has the right to say what He wants and does not want. We must not change the way God has instructed us to worship!

By studying worship, we can learn another very important lesson about authority. Sometimes the person who has the authority explains exactly what he wants; at other times he lets people use their own judgment.

For example, suppose a farmer tells his hired help to build a barn. That is the only thing he says he wants—a barn. With that type of instruction, the farmhand can use pine, oak, or poplar, he can paint the barn blue, pink, or red, and he can make it one, two, or fifty stories tall. He was simply told to build a barn. Now suppose the farmer told his worker to build a red barn, made of oak wood, twenty feet high. With these specific instructions, the worker is limited to only one kind of wood, one color, and one height. The farmer does not have to tell the worker **not** to use pine, maple, cherry, cedar, or poplar. He simply needs to say what kind of wood he wants. He does not have to list all the kinds of wood he does **not** want.

This same principle can be seen in the story of Noah's ark. God told Noah to build an ark made of gopherwood. We never read a single verse where God told Noah **not** to use pine, oak, or cedar. But Noah did not use any other wood. He used only gopher wood, because that was the kind of wood God gave him the authority to use.

In New Testament worship, the principle works the same way. For instance, when we read in the Bible about the Lord's Supper, we learn that two items were used—unleavened bread and grape juice. The apostle Paul instructs the Corinthian church (1 Corinthians 11:17-34) about taking the Lord's supper, using the bread and the "fruit of the vine" (a biblical term for juice that comes from a grape). But what if we don't like unleavened bread and grape juice? Can we use chocolate cake and Coke® instead of unleavened bread and grape juice? Certainly not! Why? Because God has told us exactly what He wants, and we do not have the authority to add to it or take from it. We can eat the unleavened bread out of a metal tray, straw basket, or dinner plate. We can drink the grape juice out of a glass container or a plastic container. We could eat the Lord's Supper in an auditorium or in a house where the congregation might be meeting. God has not told us where to eat it or what to use to serve it. He has, however, told us what items to eat and drink. When He did that, He excluded all other items. The fact that God gives specific authority for certain actions, automatically eliminates the addition of anything else.

Colossians 3:17 teaches that "whatever you do in word or deed, do all in the name of the Lord Jesus, giving thanks to God the Father through Him." What does it mean to do everything "in the name of the Lord Jesus?" Remember the illustration about the policeman who came to your house with a warrant. He told you to open the door "in the name of the law." That means that the law gives him permission to make you open the door. If we do everything "in the name of the Lord Jesus," that means we do those things that Christ gives us the permission to do. This verse again shows us that only Jesus, through the New Testament, has the authority to tell us what to do and how to live.

CONCLUSION

Throughout this book, the principle of authority will be applied. It will be used often, because most every question concerning worship, the church, and your spiritual life boils down to finding out who has the right to make the rules. In each part of worship and life that is discussed, we must determine when God has told us what He wants, and which decisions He has left up to us. In the end, we must always ask ourselves "Who has the right...?

DISCUSSION QUESTIONS?

1. What is authority? Who has been given all authority in heaven and on Earth? What are some groups to which He has delegated certain authority?

2. Where does the government get its authority to make rules (read Romans 13)? When does the authority of the government stop? Discuss some examples of rules that governments have made that they did not have the authority to make.

3. What kind of authority do parents have? Who gave them this authority? Where does their authority stop? Talk about some things that parents have the authority to do and some things they do not have the authority to do.

4. Who is the only one who has the authority to forgive sins? What happens when people teach ways to forgive sins that are not taught by Jesus? Have you obeyed Jesus' teachings about how to receive the forgiveness of sins? If not, why not?

5. Who has the authority to make rules about worship? Explain why God does not have to tell us everything not to do in worship. What does it mean to "do all in the name of the Lord?"

"Jesus said to him, 'I am the way, the truth, and the life. No one comes to the Father except through me.'"

John 14:6

Let's make sure to live our lives, not according to what "feels" right, but according to the truth that is found only in the Bible.

CHAPTER 2

WHICH WAY IS NORTH AND OTHER ABSOLUTE TRUTHS

It is really a very simple experiment that makes an outstanding point. All the people in a room stand up and close their eyes. Then everyone points to the direction that he or she **thinks** is north (pointing up does not count). When the people open their eyes, they notice that most all of them are pointing in different directions. A quick look at a compass shows that only a few of the people were right in their choice for north. Even though most of the people felt like they were pointing north, they were not. North is always north, regardless of how many people feel otherwise.

In our society today, many people say that there is no absolute right way to do things. The idea is that one way might be right for you, but not for another person. Each person does what **feels** right to him, and that **is** right for **him**. Many would say, "your way is fine for you and my way is fine for me," and everyone does what they think is right. In fact, according to this philosophy, there really is no single right way. One way is as good as another.

Many people believe and practice this in religion. They are content to believe that one religion is as good as another. They think that as long as a person is sincere in what he believes, that person is doing fine. Accordingly, the various religions, denominations, churches, and synagogues are all just different ways to get to the same place. Those who think this way do not believe that any one religion is **the** right religion. It might be the right religion for you, but it cannot be **the** right religion, because they believe there is no **one right religion or church**. Is this idea correct? Is there no real, absolute truth? Are all churches and religions just as good as another? Let's see how this idea works in real life.

ALL OR NOTHING

Suppose you meet a cute member of the opposite sex at school. After several weeks of building up your courage, you strike up a conversation. This charming person seems to like you, so the two of you exchange phone numbers. Later that week, you decide you would like to have another talk with this intriguing individual so you grab your cell phone, flip through the address book to the number and hit the call button. After several rings, you get an annoying recorded voice that says the number you have dialed has been disconnected or is no longer in service. You hang up, check your cell phone, and read the number again. It seems like the right number to you so you try again. Same annoying recorded message. After checking the number for the third time, you think that maybe the last digit in the number should be a five instead of a two. You feel sure that this will be the right number. This time someone picks up. To your surprise it is a guy with a deep voice named Freddy—wrong number. You try a couple other digits that you

feel are right, but each one turns out to be the wrong number. Finally, you give up.

So what does a wrong number have to do with absolute truth? The point is, if you do not have the number exactly right, you will never be able to talk to that person you were hoping to go out with. (Even though you thought the number was right—you felt so sure.) There is only one phone number that will get you connected. One number, that's it, no exceptions!

This idea of absolute right and wrong can be seen in your school subjects just as easily. Your math teacher puts a problem on the board that looks like this: 2 + 2 = ____. She says this is an all or nothing quiz. If you answer the problem right, you get a hundred. If you answer it wrong, you get a zero. Suppose you feel very sure that the answer is 5. Suppose the teacher goes out of the room and the entire class votes that the answer is five. Next, imagine that the history teacher comes in while the math teacher is out and explains that the answers three, four, and five should be acceptable as long as each student firmly believes that the answer he or she puts down is right. Is any answer except "four" going to be right? Absolutely not! We can all see that four is the only **true** answer.

ABSOLUTE TRUTH IN RELIGION

The same principle applies to religion. In Matthew 7: 13-14, Jesus said: "Enter by the narrow gate; for wide is the gate and broad is the way that leads to destruction, and there are many who go in by it. Because narrow is **the gate** and difficult is **the way** which leads to life, and there are few who find it." In John 14:6, Jesus boldly stated: "I am **the way, the truth, and the life**. No one comes to the Father except through Me." It really is as simple as 2+2. There is only one way to heaven, and Jesus is it.

What does that mean? It means that any person who tries to get to heaven without obeying Jesus will not get to heaven. This is hard for some people to accept, but it is the truth—the absolute truth that does not change. All those people who are trying to get to heaven through Buddha, Muhammad, the Old Testament, or countless other religions will be lost if they do not turn to Jesus and do things His way.

MORE THAN A FEELING

Many sincere people **feel** like they are doing right, but they are not. The apostle Paul is a great example of this. At one time in his life, Paul (whose name was first Saul) thought that Christians were evil and wicked. He thought they were pulling people away from the true way to heaven that he believed was found in the Jewish religion. Because of his sincere belief, he persecuted the Christians. He went to the leaders of the Jews and received letters that allowed him to throw Christians into prison. When Christians were on trial for their lives, Paul would vote that they should be killed. He sincerely believed that He was doing what God wanted him to do. In Acts 23:1, while he was speaking to the Jewish leaders, Paul said, "I have lived in all good conscience before God until this day." Paul **felt** like he was serving God. There was only one problem: he was not serving God. In fact, he was serving Satan and fighting against God, in spite of his sincere motive. He was sincere, but he was sincerely wrong.

When Christ appeared to Paul on the road to Damascus, He told him that he was sinning (Acts 9). Christ instructed him to go into the city of Damascus where he would be told what he needed to do to get right with God. Paul believed Jesus, and did exactly what he was commanded to do. After Paul prayed and fasted for three days, a man named Ananias came and told him, "Arise and be baptized, and wash away your sins, calling on the name of the Lord" (Acts 22:16). Paul did as he was instructed to do. He was immersed in water for the remission of his sins, and was added to the one true Church that belongs to Christ. Paul's sincerity did him no good until he found and obeyed the truth.

Today it is the same. Many sincere people "feel like" they are following God. Maybe they have done what their preacher or "pastor" has told them. Maybe they belong to the religion of their parents, or their boyfriend or girlfriend. These people may sincerely believe that they are doing right. But just because they are sincere, does not mean they are right. In fact, the book of Proverbs says, "There is a way that seems right to a man, but its end is the way of death" (14:12). Many religious teachings that "feel right" that may feel right are actually ways that lead to death.

FACTS VERSUS FEELINGS

Not long ago, a young preacher was talking to a lady who seemed very sincere. She believed that the Holy Spirit was working in her life. In fact, she believed that the Holy Spirit would communicate directly to her, telling her specific things that she must do. She told the young preacher an elaborate story about how the Holy Spirit had told her to go down to the local Toyota car dealership and buy a car. She said the Spirit had told her to buy a small one, and that she had to buy it that day or she would not get to buy it at all. After this long story, the lady also told how she had "been saved." What she described was not the way the New Testament teaches. After listening for a while, the young preacher tried to show her from the Bible that the Holy Spirit does not talk directly to people like He once did in the New Testament. He also showed her several verses that explain that she had not "been saved" like she thought, because she had not done what Jesus said. The lady paid very little attention to the Bible verses. In fact, she explained that she knew the Holy Spirit was working in her life because she could feel Him. The preacher tried several more times to show the lady what the Bible says. Finally, the lady said that "an argument can never beat an experience."

What did she mean when she said that an argument couldn't beat an experience? She simply meant that it did not matter what she learned from the Bible. She **felt** like the Holy Spirit was working in her life and she was going to trust her feeling rather than the Bible. Jesus described a very similar type of thinking. In Matthew 7:21-23 He said, "Not everyone who says to Me, 'Lord, Lord,' shall enter the kingdom of heaven, but he who does the will of My Father in heaven. Many will say to Me in that day, 'Lord, Lord, have we not prophesied in Your name, cast out demons in Your name, and done many wonders in Your name?' And then I will declare to them, 'I never knew you; depart from Me, you who practice lawlessness!' "

The people Jesus discussed **thought** they were doing wonderful things in His name. They **felt** like they were serving Jesus, but they were not. They had not taken the time to compare their actions with His instructions. They might have been sincere, but they were sincerely wrong. Thankfully, there is something much more reliable than feelings to guide us to heaven.

CONCLUSION

In John 8:32, Jesus explained, "And you shall know the truth, and the truth shall make you free." Later in the book of John, Jesus explained that God's Word is **truth** (John 17:17). In our lives today, we have been given God's Word—the Bible. In John 12:48, Jesus tells us that these words will judge us in the last day. At the Judgment, our lives will be compared to the **truth** found in the New Testament. If we have followed Jesus' words, we will go to heaven. If we have not followed them, regardless of how sincere we are, we will go to hell.

North is always north, 2+2 always equals four, and Jesus is the only way to get to God and heaven. Let's make sure to live our lives, not according to what "feels" right, but according to the truth that is found only in the Bible.

DISCUSSION QUESTIONS

1. Discuss some things that a person must have exactly right in order for them to work. Also discuss some things that simply do not change according to popular opinion.

2. Why is it difficult for people to accept that there is only one right way in religious matters? Why do you think Jesus was so insistent on there being only one right way? What will happen to people who do not choose to go the right way?

3. What are some ways that people try to determine truth incorrectly? What happens when everyone does what he or she "feels" is right (read Judges 17:6)? How do you think most religious people in the world today are making decisions?

4. What are the two ingredients that a person must have for his or her religion to be acceptable to God (read John 4:24)? What happens when people have the right actions, but they are not sincere (the Pharisees, for instance)?

5. Suppose a person is sincere in what he or she believes. Does sincerity excuse improper actions? Give some biblical examples to prove your answer. What does this mean for sincere people today who are not following the one way set out in the Bible?

"Then Peter said to them, 'Repent, and let every one of you be baptized in the name of Jesus Christ for the remission of sins...'"

Acts 2:38

The Bible teaches that baptism is the point where we contact the blood of Jesus that washes our sins away.

CHAPTER 3

BAPTISM*

Have you ever come into the house from playing or working and just been filthy—covered with dirt and grime from head to toe? I remember football games, mud fights, fishing excursions, hunting trips, and hay fields when my brothers and I probably came in for a meal and were barely recognizable to our mother because of layers of dirt. Have you ever come into the house looking and smelling like that?

You've entered the house. You're filthy. You're hungry and thirsty. You notice that the table is set for dinner. There are great smells coming from the kitchen, and each fancy place setting is crowned by an ice cold glass of sweet tea. You start to sit down. You reach for your glass of liquid refreshment, and your mom says, "What do you think you're doing? We're having company for dinner and before you enter this kitchen, I want you washed up from head to toe." You're hungry. You're

---

* Most of the Gospel plan of salvation is not disputed. Many religious groups teach the necessity of hearing the Gospel, believing it, repenting of sin, and confessing Jesus as the Son of God. But they incorrectly teach that baptism is not essential for salvation. So we have chosen not to address the commonly accepted teachings about salvation, and focus on baptism in this chapter.

thirsty. But you know she means business, so you grab a rag and a bar of soap and head for the sink. You set the water on warm and commence scrubbing, amazed at the amount of dirt coming off as the sink fills with brown water. You scrub your face, and the water running down into your mouth is full of sweat and dirt. You spit it out and then keep washing. Eventually you're cool and clean. You slap on some deodorant, wiggle into a fresh shirt, and think, "Wow, I sure feel a whole lot better."

That "sink session" that you just experienced has accomplished several things for you. First, and most obviously, it cleaned away the dirt and grime from your skin. Second, it refreshed and invigorated you. Third, it made you a presentable part of the family. Fourth, and lastly, it allowed you access to all the blessings of the family table.

Did you realize that just "washing up" did all of those things for you?

There is a Bible parallel to the scenario we've just described. It's baptism. That spiritual "washing up" that the Bible teaches is a necessary part of salvation. When we contact Jesus' blood through baptism the dirt and grime of sin is cleansed from our lives. It refreshes and invigorates us by giving us a new life in Christ. It gives us an identity as a member of God's family. And it gives us access to all the blessings God offers to His children.

If baptism does all these things, it must be pretty important. That's why Christians for thousands of years have taught the necessity of baptism. And yet, sadly, there are those today who minimize the importance of baptism and teach that it is not essential for salvation. We all know that there are other religious groups that do not recognize the necessity of baptism. But did you know that there are many who are members of the Lord's Church who are now suggesting that baptism may not be that important after all? They are teaching that a person can be saved without being baptized. Several well-known teachers in the Church have made public statements on the radio and in books claiming that baptism is **important** but not **essential** to our salvation. Are you surprised to learn that? If so, please consider the following statements.

NOT GOD'S TEACHING ON BAPTISM

On radio station KJAK in Lubbock, Texas, Max Lucado, a well-known author and preacher, made this statement about salvation. "Just call Him [God] Father. Just turn your heart to Him right now as I am speaking. Call Him Father. And your Father will respond. Why don't you do that? Father, I give my heart to you. I give you my sins, I give you my tears, I give you my fears, I give you my whole life. I accept the gift of your Son on the cross for my sins. And I ask you Father, to receive me as your child. Through Jesus I pray. Amen." After Max said these words, the announcer for the radio station said, "And friend, if you prayed along with Max Lucado just now, here on UPWORDS, we want to welcome you into the family of God."

After a few more comments and a brief commercial for one of Lucado's books, the announcer said, "Max Lucado returns with a special word for those who received the gift of salvation just moments ago in prayer." When Lucado came back on, he said, "I want to encourage you to find a church, I want to encourage you to be baptized, I want to encourage you to read your Bible. But I don't want you to do any of that so that you will be saved. I want you to do all of that because you are saved."

This is only one example of false teaching in the Church about baptism and salvation. But the purpose of this chapter is not to study all of those false teachings. We don't have to do that. Think about this. If we want to find a particular kind of spider, we need to know what that spider looks like. We can look on the Internet. We can find pictures and books. And we can study, so we'll know that spider when we see it. We don't have to recognize what all of the 30,000 spiders look like. We just have to know what the one we want looks like. The same is true about the Bible's teaching on baptism. We don't have to know all the false teachings about baptism. We just have to know the true teaching about it. If we are able to recognize Bible baptism when we see it, we will know the truth. If we know the true teaching, we'll also be able to recognize false teaching.

The purpose of this chapter is to study and affirm what the **Bible** teaches about **baptism**.

WHAT GOD SAYS ABOUT BAPTISM

First, the Bible teaches that baptism is necessary for salvation.

Shortly after Jesus went back to Heaven, the apostles were gathered together in Jerusalem awaiting a sign from God that would let them know what to do. The sound of a mighty wind swept through the building where they were staying and fire miraculously appeared burning over their heads. But the wind and the fire were not the only miracles that day. After the wind and fire appeared, the apostles began publicly preaching the message of Jesus to Jews who had gathered in Jerusalem from all parts of the world. Even though the many people listening spoke many different languages, each person was able to hear the apostles' teaching in his own language. Some of the listeners thought it was a joke. Some of the listeners thought the apostles were drunk. But Peter stood up and defended the apostles and preached one of the first sermons about Jesus' life, His death, His burial, and His resurrection (Acts 2:14-40).

Many of those listening to Peter's sermon had taken part in Jesus' arrest, trial, and crucifixion. These people realized the sin they had committed. They were grief-stricken and guilty. The Bible says "they were cut to the heart, and said to Peter and the rest of the apostles, 'Men and brethren, what **shall we do**?'"

Okay, stop, freeze the picture, hit your "pause button." The people in Acts 2 had just heard a sermon about Jesus' life, death, burial, and resurrection. They realized, after hearing the sermon, that there was something that they needed to do to get right with God, and they wanted to know what it was. So they asked an apostle, Peter, in fact. And he told them. But before we look at what Peter told them, let me ask you this: Who has more right to answer that question? Billy Graham, Max Lucado or the apostle Peter? Your preacher or "pastor," your youth minister, that great speaker at the youth rally Friday night or the apostle Peter? Your grandmother, your friend at school, or the Holy Spirit-inspired apostle Peter? Not a very hard question is it? We need to listen to Peter! How about you? Let's listen then. (Press your "play button" now.)

> "Now when they heard this, they were cut to the heart, and said to Peter and the rest of the apostles, 'Men and brethren, what shall we do?' Then Peter said to them, 'Repent, and let every one of you be baptized in the name of Jesus Christ for the remission of sins...'" (Acts 2:37-38).

There was a question. There was an answer. If you ask the same question today, you'll get the same answer. Why? Because the Bible teaches that baptism is essential for our salvation. Listen to some more of Peter's teaching on the subject: "There is also an antitype which **now saves us**, namely baptism (not the removal of the filth of the flesh, but the answer of a good conscience toward God), through the resurrection of Jesus Christ" (1 Peter 3:21, emphasis added).

Next, the Bible teaches that baptism is the point where we contact the blood of Jesus that washes our sins away.

Remember how Peter answered the question of the listeners on Pentecost? "Repent, and let every one of you be baptized in the name of Jesus Christ for the remission of sins" (Acts 2:38). Baptism is the point at which our sins are washed away. Not that there's anything magical or mystical about the water itself, but God works through the water for the cleansing of the sin from our soul. Baptism works, through the power of Christ's blood, for the cleansing of our souls. Saul of Tarsus, a man who would later be called Paul the apostle, was commanded by a godly teacher to "Arise and be baptized, and wash away your sins..." (Acts 22:16).

Third, the Bible teaches that baptism is the point at which we begin a new life with Christ.

Just like cool, clean water refreshes and invigorates us when we wash, baptism makes us a new creation in God's sight—a new person. The old life of sin ends. The new life for Christ begins. Jesus referred to baptism as a new birth in his conversation with Nicodemus. Jesus taught, "unless one is born again, he cannot see the kingdom of God." Nicodemus was confused and asked, "How can a man be born again?" Jesus replied, "unless one is born of water and the Spirit, he cannot enter the kingdom of God" (John 3:3-5). Paul, in more than one place, teaches how our new lives in Christ begin at baptism. Romans 6:3-4 says, "Or do you not know that as many of us as were baptized into Christ Jesus were baptized into His death? Therefore we were buried with Him through baptism into death, that just as Christ was raised from the dead by the glory of the Father, even so we also should walk in newness of life." Colossians 2: 12-13 says that we are "buried with Him in baptism, in which you also were raised with Him through faith in the working of God, who raised Him from the dead. And you being dead in your trespasses..., He has made alive together with Him, having forgiven you all trespasses." We cannot be saved unless we stop living a life of sin and start living a life with Christ. The Bible teaches that baptism is the point at which our old lives end and our new lives begin.

Last, the Bible teaches that baptism is how we get "into Christ."

Being "in Christ" is the most important place to be in the world. Consider all the things that are in Christ from Ephesians chapters one and two.

God has "blessed us with every spiritual blessing in the heavenly places **in Christ**" (1:3).

"...He chose us **in Him** before the foundation of the world..." (1:4).

"...He made us accepted **in the Beloved"** (1:6).

"**In Him** we have redemption through His blood, the forgiveness of sins..." (1:7).

"...He might gather together in one all things **in Christ**..." (1:10).

"**In Him** also we have obtained an inheritance..." (1: 11).

"...**in whom** also, having believed, you were sealed with the Holy Spirit..." (1:13).

"But now **in Christ Jesus** you who once were far off have been brought near..." (2:13).

The list goes on and on. The blessings of being in Christ are limitless. And if we want those blessings, we must be in Christ. The apostle Paul knew this was the most important truth of all, and he concluded: "I also count all things loss for the excellence of the knowledge of Christ Jesus my Lord, for whom I have suffered the loss of all things, and count them as rubbish, that I may gain Christ and be found **in Him**..." (Philippians 3:8-9).

Heard enough? Do you want to be in Christ where all these spiritual blessing are to be found? Let's see how the Bible tells us to get there! Hold your breath though, because it's fast, simple, and powerful. Here it is: "For as many of you as **were baptized into Christ** have put on Christ" (Galatians 3:27).

Did you miss it? Need to read it again? "For as many of you as were baptized **into Christ** have put on Christ."

All the good things that God gives us and promises us are in Christ, and the Bible teaches that we get into Christ through baptism.

CONCLUSION

Even though there are those who teach that baptism is not necessary for salvation, that is not what the Bible teaches. Let's teach and defend what the Bible teaches. Let's be aware of false teaching and continually study and affirm our commitment to the true Bible teaching of baptism.

DISCUSSION QUESTIONS

1. List some verses where the Bible teaches that a person must be baptized in order to be saved? What must a person understand in order to be baptized properly?

2. If the blood of Christ forgives sins (Ephesians 1:7), why then does the Bible say that a person must be baptized to be forgiven (Acts 22:16)?

3. When a person is baptized, what events in the life of Jesus are being reenacted during that person's baptism? Read Romans 6:3-6 and Colossians 2:12 to help with your answer.

4. In 1 Peter 3:21, the Bible says that baptism saves a person. In Luke 13:3 Jesus says that a person must repent to be saved. John 6:47 says that those who believe in Jesus will have everlasting life. How can all these verses be true at the same time? What would be wrong with picking out only one thing, like belief or repentance, and claiming that it was the only thing necessary for salvation?

5. What are some of the things that are found "in Christ"? How does the Bible say that a person gets "into Christ"? What will happen to a person who dies outside of Christ (read John 8:24)? What will happen to those who die in Christ (read 1 Thessalonians 4:13-18)?

"...on this rock I will build My church, and the gates of Hades shall not prevail against it."

Matthew 16:18

Is one group right and all others wrong? Who is going to Heaven? Which church is Jesus' Church? Or are they all His churches? How many churches did Jesus build?

CHAPTER 4

IS ONE CHURCH AS GOOD AS ANOTHER?

"Do you think you 'Church of Christ' folks are the only ones going to Heaven?"

Have you ever been put on the spot with that question? I have, and I bet if you've had many religious discussions with people, you have too.

What did you say? Did you stammer around not really knowing what to say? Did you find it hard to say what you really believe? You wanted to be honest, but at the same time you wanted to be fair, open-minded, and non-offensive. So what did you say?

A person looking for a church would probably just need to take a short drive down the main street of your town to find a wide variety of options. Within a few short blocks, he would probably find a couple of Baptist churches, maybe a Presbyterian church building, a Methodist church building, a Community Church, an Assembly of God, a Kingdom Hall of Jehovah's Witnesses, a Lutheran church, a Catholic church, an Episcopal church, and at least one building with a sign that says "Church of Christ." This list is by no means complete. Likely there are more religious groups than that in your town. In fact, there are more than 2,500 religious groups in the world with different beliefs. But you get the picture. How is a person supposed to choose between all the groups? Is one group right and all others wrong? Who is going to Heaven? Which church is Jesus' Church? Or are they all His churches? How many churches did Jesus build?

Straight from the Savior's Mouth

If you want to get the straight answer, you've got to go to the source. If Jesus were sitting right next to us, we could ask Him. In a way, He is right next to us. We have the very words that He taught His disciples. We can learn the answer to our question, "How many churches are there?"—"straight from the Savior's mouth," so to speak.

In Matthew 16:18, Jesus said, "...on this rock I will build My church, and the gates of Hades shall not prevail against it." How many churches did **Jesus** say **He** was going to build? **Jesus** said **He** was going to build **one** church that belonged to Him. It was not going to be built by **men**. It was not going to have man's rules and man's teaching. It was going to belong to **Jesus**, to worship **Him**, to serve **Him**, and to work and to worship according to **His** commands and teachings.

On the night of Jesus' arrest and betrayal in the garden of Gethsemane, He prayed for a very long time. He prayed for the apostles. And He prayed for everyone who would have faith in Him through the apostles' teaching—Christians today. Do you know what he prayed for you and me? He prayed that everyone who believed in His name would believe and teach the same thing. John 17:20-22 says:

> "I do not pray for these [the apostles] alone, but also for those [you and me] who will believe in Me

> through their word; that they all may be one, as You, Father, are in Me, and I in You; that they also may be one in Us, that the world may believe that You sent Me. And the glory which You gave Me I have given them, that they may be one just as We are one."

The longest recorded prayer of Jesus is for the unity of all His followers. Religious division and denominationalism is not all right with Jesus. It is **not** what He wants. He wants His people to be one, with the same unity that He and the Father have. Do you think that could happen today? Jesus knew He was asking a difficult thing, but in the same prayer He taught how such unity is possible. He asked God to, "sanctify them [believers] by Your truth. Your word is truth" (John 17:17). The Truth, God's Word, is the only thing that will unite those who believe in Christ. When men refuse to listen to God's Word and choose to add to it and subtract from it, there can be no unity. When men replace the doctrine of the New Testament with their own doctrines, there can be no unity. When men replace the name of Christ with another name, there can be no unity.

There are sincere, religious people who are going to be lost. Jesus said, "Not everyone who says to Me 'Lord, Lord,' shall enter the kingdom of heaven, but he who does the will of My Father in heaven" (Matthew 7:21). Many who believe in Jesus will be lost, because they have followed the teachings of men instead of the Lord's teaching. Many people practice an empty religion, because they have followed men's traditions instead of truth. Jesus said, "...in vain they worship Me, teaching as doctrines the commandments of men" (Matthew 15:

9). In Romans 10:2, Paul prayed for lost Jews when he said: "They have a zeal for God, but not according to knowledge." When people substitute what they want for what God wants, when they substitute men's names and teachings for Christ's, they cannot be pleasing to God.

DIVISION WAS NOT GOD'S IDEA

The word "denomination" means a division based on names. Ride down the road and observe it for yourself. Every name on a church building reflects a set of teachings or a particular tradition. Christ hates this division. He doesn't want people to divide under different names. He wants people to unite under His name.

The church in Corinth is one of the places we read of the beginnings of denominationalism. In the Corinthian church, there were many divisions. Powerful teachers in and around Corinth had taught and converted most members of the Corinthian church. The new Christians were proud that they had been taught and baptized by such popular and powerful teachers. They bragged about the teachers who baptized them, and they formed cliques within the church. The "Paul Christians" were a group; the "Peter Christians" were a group; and the "Apollos Christians" were another group. The situation was very similar to today. These "denominations" claimed to all be Christians, just different kinds of Christians. Was the Lord pleased with the Corinthian cliques? Absolutely not! In fact, Paul himself condemned such division. "Is Christ divided? Was Paul crucified for you? Or were you baptized in the name of Paul?" (1 Corinthians 1:13). The answer to all of Paul's questions is "NO!" And if we ask if denominationalism and division is pleasing to Jesus, the answer is the same—a resounding "NO!"

Many religious people would argue that denominations are good, because they let people be Christians in different ways. But we have already seen that this is not what Christ wants. He wants His people to be the same. Ephesians 4:3-6 says, "endeavoring to keep the unity of the Spirit in the bond of peace. There is one body and one Spirit, just as you were called in one hope of your calling; one Lord, one faith, one baptism; one God and Father of all, who is above all, and through all, and in you all."

Christ's own prayer was for the unity of all believers, but He knew that unity could only be built on the Truth of God's Word. When men substitute names, teachings, practices, and creeds for the true doctrine of the New Testament, there can be no unity. The result is the confusing and mixed up religious landscape we see all around us. It's called denominationalism, and Christ hates it.

IS ONE CHURCH AS GOOD AS ANOTHER?

The bumper sticker reads, "ATTEND THE CHURCH OF YOUR CHOICE." The idea is that one church is as good as another. This is America, and everybody's got the right to their own opinion. Who are you to tell me I'm wrong anyway? Sound familiar? It ought to. It's the idea that most Americans have about religious division—one church is as good as another.

But is this right? Is one church as good as another?

For an answer to this question let's look at the writing of a man named Joe T. Odle*. Mr. Odle is a denominational preacher who wrote a booklet titled the *Church Members Handbook.* In this book Mr. Odle says:

> "There are hundreds of denominations in the world today, teaching almost every conceivable kind of doctrine. They cannot all be right, for they do not all teach the same thing. Indeed, many of their teachings are in direct conflict, one church proclaiming a doctrine that another denies. Can both be right? If not, then the one that is right in its teaching must admittedly be better than the one that is wrong."

How does that sound to you? Does it make sense? But Mr. Odle does not stop there, he lists five considerations for determining if one church is better than another.

1. A church established by man is not as good as a church established by the Lord.

2. Churches that teach error are not as good as churches that teach the truth.

3. Churches that teach only part of the truth are not as good as those that teach all the truth.

4. A church whose doctrines give glory to man is not as good as one whose doctrines give all glory to God.

5. A church that refuses to obey Christ's commands and takes for doctrines the commandments of man is not as good as one whose sole authority is the Lord.

Mr. Odle concludes by saying, "We believe that a careful study of these points will convince the reader that

---

* While we would not endorse all of Mr. Odle's teachings, we do feel that he is correct in using the Scriptures as the standard for identifying the Church.

one church cannot be as good as another in the sight of the Lord." And this is the truth. One church is not as good as another. Man's teaching is not as good as God's teaching. And a man's name is not as good as Christ's name.

IF IT WALKS LIKE A DUCK...

How do you know a duck when you see one? Out of twelve different types of birds, could you recognize a duck? How? It would have a bill. It would quack and waddle on big webbed feet. It could swim and dive. In short, you would know it was a duck by the way it looked and acted.

Can we know the Lord's Church when we see it? Can we recognize the Church established by Christ? And can we recognize a man made denomination? Let me suggest a few tests to apply:

1. The Lord's Church will wear a Bible name. Most denominational groups use names that reflect the name of a human founder or a special creed or doctrine the group holds. It is unlikely that a group that does not wear a Bible name will be the Church that Christ established.

2. The Lord's Church will be organized in the Bible way. The New Testament clearly defines the way God wants His Church to be organized. Each church is to be autonomous. That means that no outside group has authority over a local church. There is no state or national headquarters. And no church has the right to tell another church what to do or how to do it. Each church is to be guided by spiritual shepherds, sometimes called elders or pastors, godly men who meet very strict qualifications listed in 1 Timothy 3:1-7 and Titus 1:5-9. These men are to lead the church. There must be more than one Shepherd in each church. Under the shepherds, other qualified men are selected to lead in different areas of the church's work. These men are called "deacons," and the Bible also provides a list of qualifications for this job (1 Timothy 3:8-13). Within the church there are also teachers, preachers, and evangelists. A church that is organized in any other way is not organized according to God's ideal pattern.

3. The Lord's Church will worship in the Bible way. Christ said that "those who worship the Father must worship Him in spirit and Truth" (John 4:24). There is a Bible way to worship. We must search the Bible to learn this Bible way. We must not add to or take away from that Bible way. If the Bible commands us to sing, we should sing. If the Bible says that the Christians took the Lord's Supper every Sunday, then we should, too (Acts 20:7). If the Bible says a woman should not teach or have authority over men, then Christian men and women should not allow this to happen (1 Timothy 2:12). A group of people that is not worshiping in the Bible way is probably not the Lord's Church.

4. The Lord's Church will teach Jesus' plan of salvation. Many denominations and religious groups teach different ways for a person to be saved. Some teach that a simple prayer to Jesus will save. Others teach that being baptized as a baby puts a person in the kingdom of God. Still others teach that sprinkling, or pouring water on a person puts them in a saved condition. The Lord's church will teach the New Testament plan of salvation. The New Testament teaches that a person must hear the message of Christ (Romans 10:17), believe that message (John 8:24), repent of his or her sins (Luke 13:3), confess the name of Jesus (Romans 10:10), be immersed in water for the forgiveness of his or her sins (Acts 2:38), and live faithfully (Revelation 2:10). Any religious group that does not teach the biblical plan of salvation cannot be the Lord's Church.

5. The Lord's Church will be busy doing the Lord's work. "By their fruits you will know them" (Matthew 7: 20). Jesus said this about being able to recognize true teachers from false ones. The Lord's people will be busy doing the Lord's work. Jesus said, "Let your light so shine before men, that they may see your good works and glorify your Father in heaven" (Matthew 5:16). A church that is not busy teaching its members Bible truth, caring for the needy and sick, spreading the Good News of Jesus to the world, defending Truth against error, helping the hurting, strengthening the weak, and guiding the confused is probably not the Lord's Church.

By applying each of these tests we should be able to distinguish the Lord's Church from denominations. Is the name a Bible name? Is the church organized according to the Bible pattern? Is the church worshipping according to the Bible? Is the church busy doing the Lord's work in His way? Many religious groups may meet some of these qualifications, but a church that does all of these is the Church that belongs to the Lord, purchased by His blood.

Is the Church of Christ a Denomination?

If you use the tests we've already discussed you can see that Church of Christ is not a denomination. "Church of Christ" is not a denominational name. It is a Bible name (Romans 16:16) that means "the Church that belongs to Christ." This is different from a denominational name. Notice how those who research and write about denominations view the Church of Christ. The following is an excerpt from Frank S. Mead's *Handbook of Denominations in the United States* that discusses the Church of Christ:

> Because **this is not a denomination** but a fellowship with no central headquarters, record keeping is very difficult.... A distinctive plea for unity—a unity that is Bible-based—lies at the heart of the Churches of Christ. It is believed that the Bible is "the beginning place," in and through which God-fearing people can achieve spiritual oneness—to "speak where the Bible speaks and to be silent where the Bible is silent" in all manners pertaining to faith and morals. Consequently, members recognize no other written creed or confession of faith.... This basic concept has resulted in such practices as weekly observance of the Lord's Supper, baptism by immersion, a cappella singing, a vigorous prayer life, support of church needs through voluntary giving, and a program of preaching and teaching the Bible. This concept also explains the autonomy of local churches, governed by elders and deacons appointed under New Testament qualifications....Churches of Christ maintain that the final judgment of all religious groups is reserved unto the Lord. This view, however, still allows for a vigorous evangelism that finds unacceptable the doctrines, names, titles, and creeds

> that have been grafted onto the original practice of Christianity (page 99).

Even the *Handbook of Denominations* correctly says the Church of Christ is not a denomination. But sadly there are those both inside and outside of the Church, who want to make it one. There are many who want to add unscriptural practices to the Church's worship practices. There are those who want to change the organization of the Lord's Church. There are others who want us to join the rest of the denominational world. And we are tempted, aren't we? To be like everybody else. To take the easy way out. To give in and conclude that everybody's okay. To say that one church is as good as another. But we know this is not right.

CONCLUSION

We must be careful not to treat the Church as if it is a denomination. Have you ever heard these phrases? "I'm Church-of-Christ," a "Church-of-Christ preacher," "He was raised Church-of-Christ." These phrases and others like them make us think of the Church as a denomination, when it is not one.

The Church that belongs to Christ has never been a denomination. It never will be. Christ built it. It should be quite easy for us to see that any church built by men is not **the** Church that Christ established.

DISCUSSION QUESTIONS

1. What would you say to a person who says that "Church of Christ" people believe that they are the only ones going to heaven?

2. There are hundreds of different religious groups who teach things that are contradictory to one another. Since we know this is the case, can all of them be teaching and doing right? How can we decide which church (or congregation) is doing and teaching correctly?

3. Is the "Church of Christ" just one of many denominations? If not, what makes it any different from denominations? In your own words, what does the Frank Mead's book about denominations say about the Church of Christ?

4. How many churches does the Bible teach that Jesus built? According to Paul's words in 1 Corinthians 1, what does the Lord think about division in the Church? What does the word "denomination" mean?

5. List and discuss the five things that a church or congregation must do in order to be the Church that Jesus died to save.

"God is Spirit, and those who worship Him must worship in spirit and truth."

John 4:24

In the Bible we read of worship that is good and right and also of worship that is false and wrong.

CHAPTER 5

WHAT IS WORSHIP?

Let's suppose you have won an essay contest at school. Your writing was superb. Not only did your essay blow away every other entry from your school, but it also won the contest at the state level. Then, much to your surprise, your essay won the national contest, beating out 50 other essays from the other forty-nine states and Puerto Rico. For this accomplishment, you win the grand prize—a $25,000 college scholarship and an all-expense-paid trip to London, England. While in London, you'll have the opportunity to visit different places of historical importance, see wonderful sights, and learn about another culture. But the grandest honor of all is that you will get to meet the Queen, an honor most citizens of England can only dream about, and here you are, an American teenager, with a chance to meet her face to face.

Your parents are thrilled about the scholarship. You're thrilled about the trip to England. But you're not real sure about meeting the Queen. Being American, you don't know much about royalty, and as person after person keeps telling you what a great honor this is, you just get more and more nervous. What do you say to the Queen? Are there rules? Do you bow or curtsy? What's expected of you? How are you supposed to act in the presence of the Queen?

Okay, you can stop imagining now. Our topic for this chapter is worship—more specifically, what is worship?—and the little exercise in imagination about the Queen has helped us to think about some important questions relating to worship. What do you say to the Creator of the Universe? Are there rules? Do you kneel or bow? What's expected of you? How is a person supposed to act in the presence of the True and Living God?

We understand that there are different expectations of behavior that depend on whom we are with. If we are with our brothers or sisters, we can behave a certain way. We act differently around our parents. We have different standards of conduct when we're around our best friends than when we're around the school principal.

GOD'S PRESENCE

Let's talk about our behavior in God's presence. When are we in God's presence? If you said, "Always," you're right. There is not one moment in our lives when God does not see our every action, hear our every word, or know our every thought. Notice David's words in Psalm 139:

> Where can I go from Your Spirit? Or where can I flee from Your presence? If I ascend into heaven, You are there; If I make my bed in hell, behold, You are there. If I take the wings of the morning, and dwell in the uttermost parts of the sea, even there Your hand shall lead me, and Your right hand shall hold me. If I say, "Surely the darkness shall fall on me," even the night shall be light about me; indeed, the darkness shall not hide from You, but

> the night shines as the day; the darkness and the light are both alike to You (Psalm 139:7-12).

God is everywhere. "The eyes of the LORD are in every place, keeping watch on the evil and the good" (Proverbs 15:3). There is nowhere we can go that we are not in God's all-knowing, all-powerful presence.

There are times, however, when we seek God's presence. We go looking for Him. We want to listen to Him or tell Him something. We understand that He already knows how we feel and what we need—but we just want to tell Him anyway. When we seek the presence of God—that's worship.

In the Old Testament, God's people needed other people to go into God's presence for them. These religious "middle-men" were called priests and prophets. The priests' job was to speak to God on behalf of the people, to offer sacrifices on behalf of the people, and to worship on behalf of the people. The prophets' job was to speak to the people on behalf of God. Priests and prophets stood between God and His people. But there were even times when the prophets and priests were not allowed in God's Presence. God's people were, in a very real sense, separated from God's presence. There was even a curtain in the temple that separated the "Holy Place," where the priests did their work, from the "Most Holy Place," where God sometimes visited.

A wonderful thing happened, however, when Jesus died on the cross. That curtain was torn in two, from top to bottom (Matthew 27:51)! God himself was saying, "I will be separate from my people no more. Come in." In Jesus, God became Man—a selfless act that removed the barriers between us and our God. Today the only

"Middle Man" that God's people need is Jesus Christ. Hebrews 6:19-20 says, "This hope we have as an anchor of the soul, both sure and steadfast, and which enters the Presence behind the veil, where the forerunner has entered for us, even Jesus, having become High Priest...." Jesus, as our High Priest, went "behind the curtain," to open the way for us into God's presence. "Let us therefore come boldly to the throne of grace, that we may obtain mercy and find grace to help in time of need" (Hebrews 4:16). Our worship is when we come into God's Presence.

THE PROPER OBJECT OF WORSHIP

Not all worship is good, though. In the Bible we read of worship that is good and right and also of worship that is false and wrong. There is the true worship of God, as in this Genesis 24:26: "Then the man bowed down his head, and worshiped the Lord." But many other times men were guilty of worshiping things that were unworthy of worship. Sometimes men worshiped idols (man-made statues like the golden calf of Exodus 32) as in Jeremiah 1:16 where the people "burned incense to other gods, and worshiped the works of their own hands." Other times men worshiped nature, like the sun, moon, or stars: "and they were worshiping the sun toward the east" (Ezekiel 8:16); "and who has gone and served other gods, and worshiped them, either the sun or moon, or any of the host of heaven, which I have not commanded" (Deuteronomy 17:3). In Romans 1:22-25, Paul said that some men have even worshiped animals: "Professing to be wise, they became fools, and changed the glory of the incorruptible God into an image made like corruptible man—and birds and four-footed animals and creeping things...and worshiped and served the creature rather than the Creator." Still other men sinfully worshiped angels according to Colossians 2:18 and Revelation 19:10. There were even times when men worshiped other men as in Acts 10:25-26. It **is** possible to worship the wrong object.

The first and second of the Ten Commandments were "You shall have no other gods before Me" and "You shall not make for yourself a carved image—any likeness of anything that is in heaven above, or that is in the earth beneath, or that is in the water under the earth; you shall not bow down to them nor serve them. For I, the Lord your God, am a jealous God..." (Exodus 20:3-5). These two commandments are still in effect today as we can see from Jesus' statement in Matthew 4:10: "You shall worship the Lord your God, and Him only you shall serve." There is only one proper object of worship, and that is God.

IMPROPER WORSHIP

Even when men worship the proper object—the one, true, and living God—there is the possibility that their worship will be improper. The Bible identifies several types of worship that are unacceptable to God. Let's look at these:

1. Worship that comes from an unrighteous life is unacceptable. Worship that is offered by hands stained with sin is unacceptable to God. In Isaiah 1:11-17, God asked the sinful Israelites if they thought he enjoyed their worship:

"To what purpose is the multitude of your sacrifices to Me? Says the Lord. I have had enough of burnt offerings of rams and the fat of fed cattle.... The new moons, the sabbaths, and the calling of assemblies—I cannot endure iniquity and the sacred meeting. Your New Moons and your appointed feasts My soul hates; they are a trouble to Me, I am weary of bearing them. When you spread out your hands, I will hide My eyes from you; even though you make many prayers, I will not hear. Your hands are full of blood. Wash yourselves, make yourselves clean; put away the evil of your doings from before My eyes. Cease to do evil, learn to do good; seek justice, rebuke the oppressor; defend the fatherless, plead for the widow."

God despises worship that comes from lives that are full of evil. We cannot live six days of the week as sinful, worldly people and then believe that God accepts our worship on Sunday. He does not—never has, never will.

2. Worship is unacceptable when it is done for the praise of men. The Pharisees of Jesus' day had this down to a science. When they gave charitable gifts of money to help the poor, they blew a trumpet in the street to make sure they had everyone's attention. When they prayed, they stood on the street corners and made long, elaborate prayers to sound good to men. When they fasted, they made their faces look pale and thin, so others would know how "religious" they were (Matthew 6:16-18). They wanted to be seen by men as religious. They sought the applause of men, not God. And they got what they wanted. But they missed out on what was most important about worship—God's approval. Many people today are still trying to appear religious and get men's attention and approval. They come to worship to be seen. Maybe they are big on bracelets, bumper stickers, t-shirts, etc. They're big on seeking man's approval for their religion, but not God's. Worship that does not seek God's approval is not acceptable to Him.

3. Worship is unacceptable when it is offered mockingly. In Mark 15, when Jesus was on trial for His life, the Roman soldiers worshiped Him. That's what the Bible says! But notice how they did it. They covered Him with a scarlet robe—the color of royalty. They put a reed into His hands as a phony scepter. They pressed a crown of thorns on His head. They knelt to Him, and said "Hail, King of the Jews." They worshiped Jesus, but they made a mockery of that worship. Do you think that was acceptable to God? Do you think there are ways to make a mockery of worship today? Consider a few possibilities: making worship a social assembly to sit with your girlfriend or chat with your best friend, making worship a time for a nap, passing notes back and forth, text-messaging, playing games, giggling and laughing, singing a song too loudly or oddly so your friends will laugh. These are ways that people can make a mockery of worship today. In the Day of Judgment I would hate to be one of those Roman soldiers who offered mock worship to Jesus, but I think it would be just as bad to be a Christian who professed to serve God but made a mockery out of worship.

4. Worship is unacceptable when it is conducted according to man's desires and not God's. We like what we like. We like a certain kind of music. We like to be entertained by movies, plays, games, songs, and big shows. And because we like all of these things, it is very tempting to bring them into worship. And if we do not understand what worship is, we might think this is okay. However, if we know that worship is first and foremost for God, we can see that it is what **He** wants that matters, not what **we** want. During Jesus' day, just like today, there were those who tried to make their own rules for worship. Jesus condemned such teaching and concluded that their worship was empty and useless, saying, "in vain they worship me, teaching as doctrines the commandments of men" (Mark 7:7). When we substitute what men want in worship for what God wants, that makes our worship unacceptable. Paul told the Colossians that sometimes men can make additions to worship that look, sound, and feel like real worship: "These things indeed have an appearance of wisdom in self-imposed religion" (Colossians 2:23). But the true test of acceptable worship is not whether it looks, sounds, or feels religious, but whether it is what God has told us to do. We cannot substitute what we want in worship for what God wants and still expect our worship to be acceptable to Him.

PROPER WORSHIP

In Jesus' discussion with the Samaritan woman at the well in John 4, He reached this conclusion about worship: "God is Spirit, and those who worship Him must worship in spirit and truth" (John 4:24). This means that the worship we offer God must be with the proper heart and attitude, and it must also be offered the way God has commanded. We can worship with the right heart, we can be excited about worshiping God, but do it in the wrong way [Paul called this having a "zeal for

God, but not according to knowledge" (Romans 10:2)]. Or we can worship in the right way but with the wrong heart or attitude (Revelation 2:1-5).

CONCLUSION

We might worship for any number of reasons. We might seek to worship God because we need something from Him. A woman in Matthew 15:25 approached Jesus "and worshiped Him, saying, 'Lord, help me.'" It is entirely proper to worship God and bring our needs and requests before Him. This is not selfish, since it admits our dependence on Him and acknowledges His care for us.

We might also seek to worship God at times when we do not know what else to do. We might find ourselves in a situation where we do not know where to turn. When we are hurt, confused, frustrated, or grief-stricken we might feel the need to seek God's throne and His help. Job, after hearing the tragic news of the loss of all of his wealth and all of his children, "arose, tore his robe, and shaved his head; and he fell to the ground and worshiped" (Job 1:20). David, at the death of his infant son, "went into the house of the Lord and worshiped" (2 Samuel 12:20). Sometimes worship can be the only thing we know to do when we don't know what else to do.

There are other times when we might see or experience something that inspires us to worship. Seeing the glory of God's creation often inspires worship. A star-filled night sky, a low-hanging full moon, the power of a thunderstorm, the magnificent view of a mountain, the Grand Canyon, Niagara Falls, or even a simple campfire. All of these things and others might move us in awe to proclaim, "My God, How Great Thou Art."

There are other times when we seek to worship God for the simple purpose of acknowledging Who He is and what He has done for us. This is not worship that comes from need, despair, or awe but is a conscious decision to give God what He deserves—our praise, our service, and our gifts. It is the humble bowing of head and heart to the Creator of the Universe. It is the conscious acknowledgement of His wisdom, power, and mercy. It is offered in accordance with His will, because it is for Him and to Him.

DISCUSSION QUESTIONS

1. What is worship? Discuss why only certain behavior is acceptable during worship. What does the Queen of England have to do with a discussion about worship?

2. Where does the Bible say that a person can go to escape from God? How should this affect the way we live our lives?

3. What was the job of a high priest? Who is our High Priest? What sacrifice did He give in order to become our High Priest? Who are supposed to be priests now on the Earth (read 1 Peter 2:5,9)? How does this differ from what some religions teach?

4. Who is the object of our worship? Knowing who the object of worship is, how should that affect the way that we do things in worship? List things that are not proper objects of worship.

5. What is proper worship? List and discuss at least five ways to offer improper worship. What will you do to help yourself worship properly?

"Let a woman learn in silence with all submission. And I do not permit a woman to teach or to have authority over a man, but to be in silence. For Adam was formed first, then Eve."

1 Timothy 2:11-13

As we answer the question about women's role in the church, we must remember who owns the Church... Since God paid for the Church, He is the only one who can make the final decisions about how it should operate.

CHAPTER 6

WHAT'S A GIRL TO DO?

You are sitting on the couch flipping through the channels with a bag of potato chips in one hand and the remote control in another. Your favorite show just ended. There is not much on the tube, but you are not quite ready for bed. As the channels all begin to look the same, you suddenly pass a very sincere looking woman who is preaching. You have seen this same woman preaching on television before. Her sermon is not what catches your attention. You stop on this channel because you are not accustomed to hearing women preach. In fact, just about the only time you have ever heard a woman preach is on TV. You grew up in the Church of Christ. In every congregation you and your family have ever attended, women did not preach, lead singing, lead prayer, teach mixed adult Bible classes, or wait on the Lord's Table. As you sit and watch this lady, you begin to wonder why other religions let women do all these things, yet you never saw women preachers in the Church of Christ.

Maybe this scenario does not describe you. Maybe you were not raised in the Church and you have always wondered why the Church "won't let women do anything." In fact, in our American culture, it is very unpopular to have leadership positions that are "off limits" to women. Many denominations and religious groups allow women to do anything that men do. Why don't women have public leadership roles in the Lord's Church?

WE MUST REMEMBER WHOSE CHURCH IT IS

As we answer the question about women's role in the church, we must remember who owns the Church. The Bible says that God bought the Church with the blood of Jesus (Acts 20:28). Since God paid for the Church, He is the only one who can make the final decisions about how it should operate. Think about this: suppose your family buys a new house. Your neighbors come over and explain that they think your house would look best if it were painted hot pink, since all the other houses in the neighborhood are hot pink. In fact, they insist that you must paint it hot pink, so that you will be like them. Do they get to decide what color your house is? Absolutely not! **They** do not own **your** house. Only the owner gets to decide.

In a similar way, God owns the Church. The blood of Jesus was a very high price to pay for the Church. Since He owns it, only God gets to decide who the leaders of the Church should be. Even if our culture insists that the Church must be like other religions, only God gets to make the decisions about who is put in leadership positions in His Church.

According to the Owner, Who Leads in Public Worship?

In the Bible, God has clearly explained that He wants men to lead in the public worship assembly. In 1 Corinthians 14, the apostle Paul wrote a long section on how public worship should be handled. In this discussion, he wrote about the "whole church" coming together in one place (14:23). In this passage, Paul is discussing the general assembly of the church, when all the church is gathered together. His discussion focuses on who should take a public role in the general assembly of the church. In 14:34-35, the Bible says, "Let your women keep silent in the churches, for they are not permitted to speak; but they are to be submissive, as the law also says. And if they want to learn something, let them ask their own husbands at home; for it is shameful for women to speak **in the church.**"

These verses are quite surprising to some people, so let's take them slow, and work backwards. The word "church" in the Bible can mean the entire group of saved people, or it can mean "an assembly." When Paul says that it is shameful for women to speak "in church," he is saying that it should not be done in the assembly, when the church comes together as a group for worship. From these verses, it is clear that a woman should not preach when the church is assembled, nor should a woman lead the church in prayer or singing. Recently, one large congregation of the Lord's Church in a large city had a woman lead a skit for their "Easter" service. Some churches have women singing solos for the entire congregation and leading public prayers. These types of public activities led by women should not take place. They go against what God has said about public leadership roles.

WHAT ABOUT BIBLE CLASS?

After reading God's Word in 1 Corinthians 14, you probably have several questions. Your first question might be in regard to Bible classes. First, you might think that since Paul was only dealing with a situation in which "the whole church" was gathered together, then that would not count in a Bible class in which the assembly of Christians is divided up into smaller groups. Could a woman teach or lead publicly in these smaller groups? If not, can a woman even talk in Bible class? Both of these are good questions. To answer them, we must go back to the Bible.

In 1 Timothy 2:11-14, the Bible says, "Let a woman learn in silence with all submission. And I do not permit a woman to teach or to have authority over a man, but to be in silence. For Adam was formed first, then Eve. And Adam was not deceived, but the woman being deceived, fell into transgression."

There are several things in this scripture that we must examine very closely. First, you probably caught that word "silence." If a woman is to learn in "silence," why do they speak in Bible class? The key to understanding that word is found in verses one and two of 1 Timothy 2, which say that we should pray for our rulers so that we can "lead a **quiet** and peaceable life in all godliness and fear." The word "quiet" in verse two is the same word that is translated "silence" in verse 11. It does not mean never saying a single word, but it means being respectful and submissive. In fact, women can (and should) sing in the assemblies (Ephesians 5:19) and confess their faith in Jesus in response to the invitation (Romans 10:9), so we know that they can say some things.

What, then, is Paul saying to the women in 1 Timothy 2? The key phrase is in verse 12: women should not teach or have authority "over a man." In a Bible class or other public settings in which a man is present, women should not be the teachers or have authority over men. Women can teach small children's Bible classes, because they are not teaching or having authority over any adult men, so they are not violating God's instructions in 1 Timothy. But they are not to teach or have authority over a grown man.

You might be asking why God wants men to be the public leaders and teachers. Is it because they are smarter than women? Absolutely not! There are many women who are smarter and could do a better job teaching than some of the men who preach and teach. Is it because men understand the Bible better? Again, that is not it. In fact, it is often the woman of the house who reads and studies the Bible more. So why does God want **men** to lead publicly in worship, teaching, and preaching?

The Bible gives us God's reason. The verses say that God created Adam first. God made man first. That is it. God decided to make man first, and because of this, He wants men to be the public leaders in the assemblies (1 Timothy 2:11-13).

Notice that this reason is not restricted to certain times or cultures. That means it did not apply only to the first century and it does not change with each culture. Adam was made first, regardless of what culture, time, or region a person might read those words; they always mean the same thing. God's reason is the same today as it was in the first century: Adam was made first.

WHAT IF?

You might be thinking the same thing that many people think after reading God's Word regarding the role of women in public teaching and worship. You might be thinking that if a man allows a woman to be the teacher, then that would be alright. What if the preacher says it is okay for a woman to stand up in the assembly and give a testimonial? What if the male teacher of a class lets a woman be the teacher? Then she would not be having authority over the man, would she? In thinking about that idea, we must remember what we learned about authority. Some things God has given people authority to do, and other things He has not. If God says that He does not want a woman to be a public teacher over a man, then no one has the authority to change God's rule. Even if a preacher or elder says that it is okay for a woman to preach in the assembly or teach a class with adult males, that does not make it acceptable. God has told us what He wants in the assembly and public teaching situations, and no one can change that.

WHAT ABOUT GALATIANS 3:27-29?

Many people who are putting women in public leadership positions in the church say that Galatians 3:28 makes their actions alright. The verse says: "There is neither Jew nor Greek, there is neither slave nor free, there is neither male nor female; for you are all one in Christ Jesus. And if you are Christ's, then you are Abraham's seed, and heirs according to the promise." Supposedly, since Paul said there is neither "male or female" in Christ, then any person can do anything in the Church, regardless of gender. This simply is not the case. Throughout the New Testament men and women are viewed differently and have different roles (read Ephesians 5:21-28 And Titus 2:2-5). Even in the Church men and women are looked on as different. For instance, an elder of the Church must be the husband (male) of one wife (female), and a deacon must also be married to a wife (1 Timothy 3:2,11). In Galatians 3:26-28, the inspired apostle Paul is simpling saying that every person in the Church is an heir of Christ, and will receive an equal reward. This passage of Scripture is discussing salvation status, not assigned duties in the Church. Paul was **not** saying that God does not make a distinction between males and females.

WHAT *CAN* WOMEN DO IN THE CHURCH?

It would be wonderful if we had a whole chapter (or even a book) to answer this question. There are so many wonderful things that young ladies and women can do in the Church. They can teach the younger children, which is one of the most important jobs in the Church. There is usually a shortage of women chaperones on youth trips. These trips provide outstanding time for one-on-one teaching opportunities. Women also are to teach other women. The Bible specifically mentions that the older women are to teach and admonish the younger women (Titus 2:4). The list of jobs and opportunities for women in the Church could go on for pages and pages. Many women seem to be blessed with a natural sensitivity that makes them perfectly suited for organizing support for families in times of death or sickness, taking food to relatives on such occasions, and sending cards. Women can attend the nursery, greet visitors at the door, prepare the Lord's Supper trays, host baby and wedding showers, show hospitality and many more things. Women have not been left out when it comes to service in the Kingdom.

CONCLUSION

God owns the Church, and He has told us that **men** should lead in public worship and be elders and deacons. This is not because men are smarter or more intelligent. It is not because they are worth more to God. It is simply because God created Adam first. No matter how our culture says the Church should do things, only God has the right to determine who does what. God bought the Church with the precious blood of His Son. He owns the Church and knows what is best for it. Let's make up our minds to do what God wants done.

DISCUSSION QUESTIONS

1. Who owns the Church? What was the cost to buy the Church? What rights does the Owner have over the Church?

2. What group of people does the Bible teach should lead in public worship? What Scriptures teach that? What group does the Bible say should be the public teachers in mixed adult classes? What Scriptures teach that?

3. What specific reason does God give for wanting the **men** to be the public leaders and teachers? Does the Bible indicate that men should be leaders because they are smarter or better teachers? Explain your answer.

4. Which qualifications for elders and deacons would rule out a woman for the position? What does Galatians 3:27-29 actually teach?

5. List and discuss several things that women can do to help the Church and be of service in the Lord's Kingdom. Use some examples from the Bible and come up with some of your own.

"Let the word of Christ dwell in you richly in all wisdom, teaching and admonishing one another in psalms and hymns and spiritual songs, singing with grace in your hearts to the Lord."

Colossians 3:16

It all boils down to this—God told us what He wants from us. He wants us to use our voices and our hearts to worship Him in song.

CHAPTER 7

TO PLAY OR NOT TO PLAY?

THAT IS THE QUESTION.

I love music. I mean I'm not one of those really talented musical guys, but I do love it. And I love all kinds of music. Country, Rock, Pop, Rap, R&B, Classical, Broadway, Opera, Easy Listening. I just like good music, whatever it is. One of the very first things I remember really, really wanting was a guitar. When I was in first grade I wanted a guitar so badly that I could taste it. My parents told me if I made straight A's on my report card they would buy me one. So I worked as hard as a little first grader can work. I made the grades. And I still remember my Dad taking me to a pawn shop to make the special purchase.

In my memory, that pawn shop was the musical center of the universe. I seem to recall thousands of guitars in all colors and sizes (although there were probably only a few beat up old instruments). My Dad handled several. He let me handle several. Together we chose a used, acoustic Al Hombra guitar. It must have been some unknown brand, because I've never seen one since. I don't remember what it cost, but to me it was the most beautiful thing in the world. I took it home and held it and admired it. Dad tuned it. And I started to learn to play...and then quit. I never learned to play the first song. Since then I've tried the recorder (an instrument like a flute) in sixth grade, eventually mastering "Hot Cross Buns," "Mary Had a Little Lamb," and "Row, Row, Row Your Boat," but nothing else. As an adult, I bought a harmonica. They say you can learn to play the harmonica in ten hours. I worked about an hour and a half and quit. Maybe one day....

Why do I describe to you my painful memories of personal musical failure? Because I want you to know that I think music is one of the greatest things in the world. It speaks the deepest language of the soul. To me, people who play instruments are so blessed. What's cooler than a guy who can sit down with a guitar and pick and sing all night? What's more lovely than a girl who can sit down at a piano and play beautiful music? I'd settle for just being able to take a harmonica out at a campfire and being able to play "Rocky Top." I love music, and I love musical instruments.

The truth is, however, when it comes to worshiping God, it's not about what I want. It's about what God wants. And we know what He wants, because He has told us in His Word. We should be very careful then to find out what He has told us He wants. And when we find that, we must be careful to give Him just that—what **He** wants, not what we want.

AN OLD TESTAMENT EXAMPLE ... OR TWO...

Nadab and Abihu were two of the most fortunate young men in the whole Israelite camp. Their father, Aaron, was famous, powerful, and important. He was perhaps the second most important man in the world during his time. He was the brother of the mightiest prophet and leader the world had ever known—Moses. Truth be told, Aaron might have been smarter, wittier, and more popular. All this made Nadab and Abihu, Aaron's sons, very important, very powerful, and very famous, too. In fact, God singled out Nadab and Abihu to be the first priests of Israel. Their dad, Aaron, was high priest. But after, him and Moses, they were next in line to be great leaders in Israel. And Aaron and Moses were old. Nadab and Abihu were the future of Israel. They had big dreams, big plans, and big opportunities.

But the two boys' futures were cut tragically short when God killed them by sending a fire that burned them up.

Why did God do that?

Here's why: because Nadab and Abihu offered in worship to God something that He had not commanded.

Leviticus 10:1-2 says: "Nadab and Abihu, the sons of Aaron, each took his censer and put fire in it, put incense on it, and offered profane fire before the Lord, which He had not commanded them, so fire went out from the Lord, and devoured them, and they died before the Lord."

God told Nadab and Abihu what kind of fire He wanted. He did not tell them what kind of fire He didn't want. He didn't have to, because if God says He wants a certain kind of something, that particular "something" is the only thing He has authorized.

Nadab and Abihu did not give God what He commanded. They gave Him something else. They gave Him what they wanted to give—not what He said He wanted from them. Maybe they had a big, bright idea. Maybe it was easier or more convenient to give God a different kind of fire. Maybe they thought the fire they offered was better. Whatever the reason, God took their lives because they offered Him something other than what He had asked (Leviticus 10:1-2).

Let's look at another example. Saul, the first king of Israel, was given wealth, position, and military success by God. Anything that a man could need or want was at Saul's disposal. All he had to do was lead God's people the way God wanted. As a special part of God's work for Saul, He commanded him to go and annihilate a sinful nation of people called the Amalekites. The command was this: Wipe out the Amalekites. Destroy every man, woman, child, and animal. The wickedness of the nation is so great, that I want the earth wiped clean of their presence. "No problem," So Saul set about this task. The Amalekites were extremely wealthy. They had huge flocks of high quality animals—oxen, sheep, and goats. The Amalekite king, Agag, was a giant of a man, proud and ruthless. And Saul's soldiers came up with a brilliant idea. They suggested carrying all these fabulous war trophies back to Israel instead of destroying them. Perhaps they thought they could sacrifice these things to God (and maybe keep a few as well). They might have thought that they could put Agag on display and then put him to death in a public triumph. All this sounded like a pretty good idea to Saul, so he gave in. Instead of doing what he knew God had commanded, he came up with a plan that was not exactly what God wanted, but it was pretty close, maybe even a little better—Saul thought.

God's prophet Samuel met Saul on the return journey. He was furious and announced that because of Saul's disobedience God was going to take away his crown and his throne. God was angry. Why? Because Saul gave God what Saul wanted God to have and not what God said He wanted.

GOD WANTS OBEDIENCE MOST

These two similar stories point to the same conclusion—when God says He wants something, that's what He wants. He doesn't want us to second guess Him. He doesn't want us to come up with a "better" way. He does not want us to give Him something we think might be okay God wants what He said He wants. Listen to God's teaching following the deaths of Nadab and Abihu: "By those who come near Me I must be regarded as holy; and before all the people I must be glorified" (Leviticus 10:3). After Saul's disobedience Samuel asked, "Has the Lord as great delight in burnt offerings and sacrifices, as in obeying the voice of the Lord? Behold, to obey is better than sacrifice, and to heed than the fat of rams. For rebellion is as the sin of witchcraft, and stubbornness is as iniquity and idolatry" (1 Samuel 15:22-23).

Doing what God says is very important. Giving God what He says He wants is how we honor Him. That is better than our own bright ideas, better than our own design for worship—when God says He wants something from us, that is what we ought to give Him.

THE INSTRUMENTAL MUSIC DEBATE

One of the most distinctive characteristics of the Church of Christ is the refusal to worship God using musical instruments. Why this refusal? What's so wrong with instrumental music in worship? Simply this: not one page of Scripture indicates that a New Testament Christian ever once worshiped God using instruments. Not one. Not one New Testament Christian is recorded to have played an instrument in worship. In fact, instruments were not introduced into Christian worship for hundreds of years after it was established. They are an addition. They're somebody's bright idea. Somebody thought they sounded better than just plain singing, so they added them. They've been doing it ever since. And now even some churches of Christ are adding instruments.

The problem is that this is not what God said He wanted.

Here are several of the passages in the New Testament relating to music and Christian worship.

"But at midnight Paul and Silas were praying and singing hymns to God, and the prisoners were listening to them." Acts 16:25

"What is the conclusion then? I will pray with the spirit, and I will also pray with understanding. I will sing with the spirit, and I will also sing with understanding." 1 Corinthians 14:15

"speaking to one another in psalms and hymns and spiritual songs, singing and making melody in your heart to the Lord." Ephesians 5:19

"Let the word of Christ dwell in you richly in all wisdom, teaching and admonishing one another in psalms and hymns and spiritual songs, singing with grace in your hearts to the Lord." Colossians 3:16

"Is anyone among you suffering? Let him pray. Is anyone cheerful? Let him sing psalms." James 5:13

Notice anything in common about the verses above? Here are a few things. First, every one of them is a command to sing, or is an example of Christians singing. Next, there is no mention—none—of any mechanical instrument. The only instruments mentioned are our voices and our hearts. Considering the fact that the Jews often used musical instruments in worship, the fact that the New Testament eludes them is very important.

Someone might say, "People in the Old Testament used instruments." It's true. They did. But they also married multiple wives, killed their enemies with swords, and offered animal sacrifices. The Old Testament is no place to find authority for Christian worship.

Someone else might say, "Well, what about heaven? In Revelation, we read about trumpets and harps, don't we?" That's true too. But let me ask you this: Have you read Revelation? Revelation is full of symbolism. The incense is a symbol. The crowns and robes are symbols. The lamps and lampstands are symbols. Revelation speaks primarily in a symbolic way. Furthermore, Jesus explained to the Sadducees that humans and angels have not been given the same set of rules (read Matthew 22:29-30). The angels in the book of Revelation cannot be used to find authority for instrumental music in Christian worship.

CONCLUSION

It all boils down to this—God told us what He wants from us. He wants us to use our voices and our hearts to worship Him in song.

He also told Noah, Nadab and Abihu, and Saul what He wanted from them. Those who gave God something other than what He commanded were severely punished. Those who wished to honor and glorify God gave Him what He requested.

Which will we be? Will we substitute what we think might be okay for what the Bible says? Will we substitute what we think sounds better for what the Bible says? Will we give God what He wants?

It is our prayer that all God's people will honor Him by giving Him exactly—no more than and no less than—what He wants.

DISCUSSION QUESTIONS

1. Describe the position of Nadab and Abihu in Israel. Why did they get burned to death by God? What reason did God give for killing them? Does God still demand obedience of us today, or has He "lightened up" since the Old Testament? (Read 2 Thessalonians 1:6-8.)

2. When God asks for something particular, why does He not have to list all the other things that He does not want? What kind of wood did He ask Noah to use on the ark? What does it mean to obey God?

3. Why did God rebuke Saul? What were Saul and the people thinking about doing with many of the cattle they had kept? In your own words, explain God's answer to Saul and the Israelites about their "good" idea.

4. Some people claim that people in the Old Testament used mechanical instruments and thus so can Christians. What is wrong with this argument? Some say that angels in Revelation use instruments, therefore Christians can as well. What two things are wrong with this argument?

5. After reading the verses in the Bible that mention music in worship, what does the New Testament say God wants Christians to do? What is missing from each of these verses? How many verses in the New Testament give an example of a Christian playing an instrument in worship to God? In the area of music, if we want to give God exactly what He has asked for, what will we do?

"And as they were eating, Jesus took bread, blessed it and broke it, and gave it to the disciples and said, 'Take, eat; this is My body.'"

Matthew 26:26

Many times, the most difficult part of the Lord's Supper is blocking all the worldly thoughts from your mind and remembering Jesus.

CHAPTER 8

THE LORD'S SUPPER: DON'T FORGET TO REMEMBER

The smell of ribs and chicken on the grill fill the hot summer air with a delicious aroma. Canned sodas covered with ice float in a cooler on the porch just waiting for someone's hand to fish them out. A ripe red watermelon rests on the picnic table with a spoon stabbed in the center. Ah, the Fourth of July—one of America's favorite outdoor holidays. And in the midst of all of the barbeque, watermelon, and family get-togethers, one of the most exciting elements of the day has not even been mentioned—the fireworks.

In all the excitement, sometimes it is difficult to remember what the Fourth of July is really all about. If someone asked you why we celebrate the Fourth, could you tell them why our country has marked the Fourth of July as a special holiday? Could you explain that on July fourth, 1776, our founding fathers signed the Declaration of Independence, which stated that the United States was separating from Great Britain? In fact, the Fourth of July is designated as a holiday in order for Americans to remember those founding fathers and to remember how brave they were to declare their independence. Isn't it easy to forget why we do some things?

Now let's think about a Sunday morning worship service in the middle of the summer just before you go on vacation. You are looking forward to a fun-filled trip to Florida complete with food, sand, and sun. On this Sunday, the Lord's Supper comes directly after the sermon. The men serving the communion stand up front and bless the bread. As it is being passed around, it comes to you. You pinch off a small piece as you do every Sunday, pop it in your mouth and...and what? What happens when you put that tiny little piece of cracker in your mouth? Where does your mind go? Do you focus your mind on the purpose of the Lord's Supper, or do we forget the reason for the bread and grape juice?

JESUS INSTITUTES THE SUPPER

The night before Jesus was betrayed, tried, and crucified, He ate the Passover feast with His twelve apostles. Often called the Last Supper, Jesus gathered with His tiny band of devoted followers in the upper room and explained that He was soon to be betrayed. In the middle of this sad occasion, Jesus "took bread, blessed and broke it, and gave it to the disciples and said, 'Take, eat; this is My body.' Then He took the cup, and gave thanks, and gave it to them saying, 'Drink from it, all of you. For this is My blood of the new covenant, which is shed for many for the remission of sins' " (Matthew 26: 26-28). Luke informs us that Jesus also told the apostles to "do this in remembrance of Me." Jesus' purpose for giving us the Lord's Supper was to give us a reminder of His sacrifice, death, and resurrection.

THE MECHANICS OF THE SUPPER

What Should We Eat and Drink?

As we focus on the Lord's Supper, we have to ask ourselves several questions. First, we must determine what items were actually used in the Lord's Supper. There is a push in many denominations today, and in the Lord's Church, to claim that Jesus did not use unleavened bread. In fact, many are claiming that it does not matter what kind of bread is used for the Lord's Supper. Those who teach this believe that table bread, rolls, Italian bread, or any other kind of bread can be used for the Lord's Supper. Was the bread at the Supper regular loaf bread? Was it special garlic toast? What kind of bread did Jesus use? And what kind of bread should we use today?

From the Bible, there is absolutely no question what kind of bread Jesus used in the Lord's Supper. He used unleavened bread—bread with no yeast in it. How do we know that? First, we know that Jesus ate the Last Supper with His disciples on the first day of the Passover feast when the Passover lamb was supposed to be killed (Mark 14:12). Second, we know that during the feast, it was unlawful for any leaven to be found in the houses of Israelites (Exodus 12:15). In fact, any Israelite who ate leaven during this feast was to be "cut off from Israel" (this phrase often meant being put to death). Eating leavened bread during the Feast of Unleavened Bread was a very serious offense. Finally, we know that Jesus was born "under the Law" of Moses and fulfilled it (Galatians 4:4). Therefore, we know Jesus used unleavened bread. As for the drink that Jesus used, it is a fact that Jesus used grape juice. The phrase "fruit of the vine" in the Bible is used to describe juice from grapes. So, if we want to follow the example of Jesus, we must use unleavened bread and grape juice. We cannot use pizza crust and water, or Italian bread and soda. Jesus' example is clear.

When Should We Eat It?

As you talk to people in different denominations, you will soon discover that many of them take the Lord's Supper only a few times a year, or once every month. Does the New Testament give us an example as to how often we should take the Supper?

Acts chapter 20:7 teaches, "Now on the first day of the week, when the disciples came together to break bread...." The phrase "to break bread" is a phrase that is used in this verse to refer to the Lord's Supper. This verse explains that a purpose for the Christians coming together was "to break bread." The Lord's Supper was a main reason they came together on the first day of the week. Which "first day of the week" was this? Was it the first one of the month, a special Christmas service, or a bi-monthly get together?

In the book of 1 Corinthians, Paul answered several questions regarding things that were happening during worship in the church at Corinth. One of those things that needed to be addressed was the Lord's Supper, another was the way the church was giving. In 1 Corinthians 16:2, Paul explained that the church needed to do their giving "on the first day of the week." The Bible shows that the Christians met on each first day of the week.

The purpose of that meeting, among other things, was to eat the Lord's Supper and to give.

Think about it like this. Suppose that you work for a company where you get paid on Friday. Does that mean you get paid on Friday twice a year, once a month, or on special occasions during Christmas? No, it means you get paid every Friday. In the same way, the Christians in the Bible met on every first day of the week to eat the Lord's Supper.

Have We Been Doing It All Wrong?

There are those in the Church today who are claiming that the Church of Christ has been eating the Lord's Supper all wrong for the past several years. Those who teach this go to 1 Corinthians 11 to find "support" for this idea. In 1 Corinthians 11, Paul had to set the Corinthian church straight about the Lord's Supper. It seems that the Lord's Supper was being eaten in the middle of a full meal. During this meal, many of the richer brethren in the church were bringing lots of food and eating as much as they wanted. Many of the poorer brethren in the church were being intentionally neglected. Paul informed them that these wrong attitudes and actions were not supposed to be part of the Lord's Supper. In fact, he told them, "when you come together in one place, it is not to eat the Lord's Supper." They were claiming to eat the Lord's Supper, but due to their incorrect actions, it had been turned into something other than the Lord's Supper.

Paul then explained to the Corinthians that he received from Jesus the same pattern that we read in the gospel accounts. Jesus, on the night He was betrayed, took the bread, gave thanks, and passed it to His disciples instructing them to eat "in remembrance" of Him (11:23-26). Paul also explained that Jesus did the same thing with the fruit of the vine.

Those who are claiming that the Church has been taking the Lord's Supper incorrectly believe that we should make it more like a meal. They believe that taking a small bite of bread and tiny cup of grape juice is not following the New Testament example found in 1 Corinthians 11. In fact, those who teach this idea believe that the Lord's Supper will be more meaningful if we go back to eating it during a meal, all gathered around a table. Is that true? Has the Church been eating the Lord's Supper incorrectly?

As we finish with 1 Corinthians 11, you should be able to see for yourself. After Paul scolded the church for their failure to eat the Lord's Supper properly, he explained to them that the purpose was not to eat a meal and get full. In fact, he told the brethren, "if anyone is hungry, let him eat at home, lest you come together for judgment." Since the Corinthian brethren were approaching the Lord's Supper as a meal in which to feed their bellies, they were going about it all wrong. Paul tried to get them to see that taking the Lord's Supper "in remembrance" of Christ is the point of the Lord's Supper. Eating a big meal was distracting the Corinthians from that purpose, so Paul told them not even to attempt to use the Lord's Supper as a meal to fulfill their appetite. If they wanted to do that, they could eat somewhere else. The Lord's Supper is for coming together as a church to remember the Lord.

In the Church today, the Lord's Supper has been arranged to fulfill Paul's instructions. There is no doubt that when the unleavened bread and fruit of the vine are passed, they are not designed to fulfill any physical appetite. The tiny portions help us to follow Paul's instruction, and help us to remember that we are not eating these things to get full. We are eating the Lord's Supper to remember Jesus' sacrifice, exactly as God told the Corinthians to do.

It is true that it sometimes seems that the Lord's Supper is hurried and rushed so that the service can get over more quickly. And it is also true that congregations might need to think about giving the Lord's Supper more attention and time. But it is not true that taking the Lord's Supper during a meal is the answer to making it a "more spiritual" activity. From what we read about the Corinthian church, turning the Lord's Supper into a meal to satisfy physical hunger distracts from the real purpose—to remember Jesus.

In Spirit...

In John 4:24, Jesus explained that those who worship God must worship Him in "spirit and truth." He meant that the outward actions must be what God commands, and the worshipers' "spirit" must also take part in the worship. Have you ever finished taking the Lord's Supper and realized that you were so busy thinking about that vacation, the girl or boy sitting beside you, or that upcoming soccer game, that you did not even stop to think about Jesus and His sacrifice on the cross? You were eating the Lord's Supper, but your "spirit" did not participate. While it is important to eat unleavened bread and to drink grape juice on the first day of the week, those things are not really the most difficult parts about the Lord's Supper. Many times, the most difficult part of the Lord's Supper is blocking all the worldly thoughts from your mind and remembering Jesus—thinking about the pain, agony, and humiliation He suffered on the cross for you and me. In the end, the real challenge is to eat the Lord's Supper "in remembrance" of Christ.

CONCLUSION

The next time you put that tiny piece of unleavened bread in your mouth, and sip down that cup of grape juice, don't forget to remember Jesus' hanging on that cruel cross praying, "Father, forgive them for they know not what they do" (Luke 23:34).

DISCUSSION QUESTIONS

1. What does the Bible say is the purpose of the Lord's Supper? When was the Lord's Supper first instituted? When did the first century church meet to take the Lord's Supper?

2. How do we know what kind of bread was used for the Lord's Supper in the first century church? What was the drink used in the Supper? Why do you think God gave us physical emblems like unleavened bread and grape juice for the Lord's Supper?

3. What were some of the problems that the church in Corinth was experiencing when taking the Lord's Supper? How did Paul tell them to fix these problems? What did Paul explain was not the purpose of the Lord's Supper?

4. What does it mean to worship "in spirit?" In your own experience, what has been the most difficult part about taking the Lord's Supper properly? What will you do in the future to help you worship in spirit and in truth in regard to the Lord's Supper?

5. Why do you think that it is so easy to forget such important things like the signing of the Declaration of Independence, and especially the death of Christ? What could a congregation do to help its members remember Jesus more during the Lord's Supper?

"Therefore I desire that the men pray everywhere, lifting up holy hands, without wrath and doubting..."

1 Timothy 2:8

Worship is not designed for us to be entertained. It is designed for God to be glorified.

CHAPTER 9

"HAND CHECK"

Have you ever been riding on a bus on a Friday night going to a youth rally or retreat, sitting beside that cute member of the opposite sex that you were dating? Maybe you were holding hands, and the youth minister or one of the chaperones yelled "hand check." When one of the adults yells "hand check" on a youth trip, that means that all hands must be shown, just to make sure that no one is holding hands, which, of course, is not permitted on the bus to youth rallies or retreats. Maybe you got busted and the little kid in front of you had a great time snickering about it.

The "Hand Checks" were annoying and embarrassing, but in all reality, they were probably not a bad idea. Sometimes everyone needs someone to check up on them. Sometimes we need to have a "hand check." There is much false teaching coming into the church today concerning the use of our hands. There is a great deal of controversy over the use of our hands in worship in these two areas especially: hand clapping and lifting up holy hands. You've probably seen some of this or experienced it at a church assembly or youth rally. Maybe it made you feel awkward. Maybe it made you feel great. But no matter how it made you feel, we need to study the Bible on these matters to determine how we should respond when these things occur.

Let's have a worship "Hand Check."

HANDCLAPPING

Hand clapping in a church assembly usually occurs in one of two forms: 1) applause as a sign of approval for a person's words or actions; and 2) musical clapping in the course of a song. Let's deal with both.

As applause

The dictionary defines "applause" as "to express approval especially by clapping the hands." Many times following a lesson, a presentation, or a baptism, a group of people will applaud as a sign of their praise or approval. This is very natural for us. We applaud everything. At a school play, we applaud. At a ball game, we applaud. Following any award presentation, we applaud. We applaud things we don't even feel deserve applause. We do it because in our society it is expected.

We need to answer a few questions about handclapping as applause:

1. Does the New Testament ever mention the use of handclapping as applause in worship?

2. How did the church in the Bible express their approval or encouragement?

The first question is one that should be asked of anything done in worship. Does the New Testament ever mention handclapping in its examples and instructions about worship? The very simple answer is no. There is not a single verse that says the New Testament church ever clapped their hands as applause or encouragement in worship. Why do we sing? The Bible says we should. Why do we pray? The New Testament tells us to. Why would we clap our hands? The New Testament does not give an example of it, nor does the Bible tell Christians to do it. That means that the idea must have come from somewhere other than the New Testament. In fact, the idea came from our culture, not the Bible.

Second, we should consider how those in the New Testament expressed approval and encouragement during worship. The Bible shows us at least three ways the New Testament church expressed encouragement and approval in worship.

1. By saying “Amen.” The English word “amen” comes from a Greek and a Hebrew word that means “let it be so.” In both the Old and New Testaments, God’s people would say “amen” following a reading of the law or a prayer. This was how they verbally participated in the event. In 1 Corinthians 4:16 we find the use of “amen” as a common practice in the worship of the church. And later, in Revelation, we read that heavenly beings give their praise to God using the same word (Revelation 5: 14).

2. God’s people expressed their praise and joy through singing and prayer. The cast down but unconquered Paul and Silas in the Philippian jail expressed their joy through “praying and singing hymns to God” (Acts 16:25). Notice the church’s prayer of joy in Acts 4:23-31. James 5: 13 shows that singing is a biblical way to express joy and approval: “Is anyone cheerful? Let him sing psalms.” That is why many Christians follow a baptism with a song of praise or a prayer of praise and thanksgiving.

3. Through preaching and teaching, the New Testament writers and leaders expressed their approval and encouragement. Ephesians 4:29 says, "Let no corrupt communication proceed out of your mouth, but what is good for necessary edification, that it may impart grace to the hearers."

In our world of "entertainment-thinking" we clap our hands to applaud many things, and by doing so we are basically saying, "we like that." In the church, however, our praise should be directed at God. Saying "amen" should not mean that "we like that" but it should mean that what has been said is right and in accordance with God's will. Again, it makes no difference whether we "like" something that is said, only whether it is true and right. We must never treat worship like a ball game or other form of worldly entertainment, where we clap and applaud actions we like. (Would we boo and hiss something we didn't like?) Worship is not designed for us to be entertained. It is designed for God to be glorified. Handclapping as applause often causes people to loose focus of the purpose of worship.

Handclapping as Musical Accompaniment

Handclapping is also used as a musical accompaniment in some songs. We are not talking about little kids' songs with a clap or two in them. "If you're happy and you know it clap your hands" doesn't have one word about God in it. And the "crash" that accompanies the foolish man's house falling down is hardly rhythmic accompaniment. We are referring to the use of clapping to simulate a musical instrument—clapping that in all practicality becomes a musical instrument. Again, we must ask if the New Testament ever mentions handclapping as musical accompaniment. The answer, once again, is simply no. The New Testament never gives a single example or instruction about handclapping as musical accompaniment.

Can we clap our hands together to make the sound of an instrument? To answer that, we must remember what kind of music God requested from us. God told us that He wants us to sing. When we add things like handclapping, we are including something that God has not asked for, which is always dangerous. There is practically no difference between clapping our hands as accompaniment, and using a musical instrument. In both cases, we are adding a "musical" sound we like to enhance the singing, or to make it more enjoyable for us. Yet, even though we might feel like the singing has been "enhanced" or made more enjoyable, God does not necessarily feel the same way. The only way to make sure that God is satisfied with our worship is to give Him exactly what He has requested from us.

LIFTING UP HANDS

A recent trend in many churches is the raising of hands during singing or prayer. Most often those who raise their hands will sway from side to side in rhythm to the music, or close their eyes as they sing and pray. Denominations have been practicing this for many years. And there are those in the Church who are teaching that all New Testament Christians should "lift up" their hands in prayer and song. This teaching is based on one New Testament verse—1 Timothy 2:8, which says, "I desire therefore that the men pray everywhere, lifting up holy hands, without wrath and doubting."

What is this verse saying? Is it literal or is it figurative? Is Paul talking about literally raising our hands or is he using a figure of speech? Is this a command to pray with upraised arms?

Consider this verse carefully. Let's suppose we take this verse literally. Let's suppose we feel that this is a command to pray with upraised arms. Does this mean we cannot pray in other ways? The Bible specifies many prayer postures—the most common of which is kneeling. But at other times, Bible characters stood to pray. Sometimes those who prayed raised their eyes to heaven. Sometimes they bowed their heads. Sometimes those who prayed laid face down, as Jesus did in the garden of Gethsemane. Paul encouraged the Thessalonians to "Pray without ceasing" (1 Thessalonians 5:17); most take this to mean that we can pray anywhere—driving down the road, standing in line at the grocery, or lying in bed at night. It is obvious that the prayer posture of our bodies is optional, with this exception: we should never pray in such a way as to draw attention to our "spirituality." Jesus condemned the Pharisees for their showy prayers (Matthew 6:5-6). We want to have God's attention, not everyone else's. And what gets God's attention is the posture of our **heart,** not our **hands**.

Back to 1 Timothy 2:8. Who are encouraged to lift up hands? Well, if we take the verse literally, he's talking to men—not women. He tells the women how to conduct themselves in the next few verses; "in like manner also, that the woman adorn themselves in modest apparel, with propriety and moderation, not with braided hair or gold or pearls or costly clothing, but which is proper for women professing godliness, with good works. Let a woman learn in silence with all subjection. And I do not permit a woman to teach or to have authority over a man but to be in silence" (1 Timothy 2:9-11). If you take the "lifting up holy hands" literally, then you must admit that it is only for the men. Women are commanded to do other things. It is also interesting that many of the same people who are teaching the "lifting of hands" are also pushing for women to take leadership roles in church assemblies. And what about singing? The verse does not say anything about lifting hands during singing. This verse, taken literally, **commands all men**, **not women** to lift up hands during **prayer only**.

But the fact, is this verse about lifting up holy hands should most likely be understood figuratively. What is important is not that our hands are raised but that our hands are **holy**! Is this literal or figurative? The hands referred to in this passage are holy and free from doubt and anger. Hands are represented throughout the Bible as symbols of a lifestyle. Psalm 24:3-4 asks: "Who may ascend into the hill of the Lord? Or who may stand in His holy place? He who has clean hands and a pure heart." Will clean hands get you into heaven? James 4:8 says: "Draw near to God and He will draw near to you. Cleanse your hands, you sinners; and purify your hearts, you double-minded." There's no soap in this world that will wash off the grime of sin. When we lift up holy hands to the Lord we are coming into His presence bearing the gift of a holy life. He doesn't care where our hands are, but He does care that our lives are free from the stain of sin.

Lifting up hands during singing and prayer is a trend. It is another attempt to make Christian worship more like an entertaining concert. It focuses on the external (hands) and not on the internal (heart). If you want to raise your hands to God in a sincere prayer, there would be nothing wrong with that. But that posture is no more acceptable than any other. And by all means don't lift up those hands as an outward show of spirituality, or because everyone else around you is doing it.

CONCLUSION

The issues of handclapping and raising hands are becoming hot topics at many youth rallies and on many college campuses. We must make sure that we know and understand the New Testament teaching on these issues. Let's simply do what God has requested from us, and not worry about fitting in with the "religious" world.

DISCUSSION QUESTIONS

1. Discuss the primary ways that handclapping is used in some worship services. What does the New Testament say about handclapping as a sign of approval in worship? Contrast worship with cultural entertainment.

2. What are some of the dangers of handclapping as applause or approval? Discuss the ways that the New Testament church showed approval and encouragement in their assemblies. What should the term "amen" mean when used in an assembly?

3. List some of the arguments that apply to the use of musical instruments as well as to handclapping as a form of musical accompaniment. What does the New Testament say about this form of handclapping?

4. Describe how you have seen people "lifting up holy hands." What verse in the Bible do many people use to support lifting up hands? If the verse is taken literally, what does that mean for men? Women? Lifting hands during singing?

5. In the Bible, what figurative use does the term "hands" often have? List some verses that support your answer. List and discuss some other prayer postures in the Bible. Why do you think many of those (like kneeling) aren't used in many assemblies today?

"For they love to pray standing in the synagogues and on the corners of the streets, that they may be seen by men. Assuredly, I say to you, they have their reward."

Matthew 6:5

When we approach God in worship, He makes the rules and says when they apply.

CHAPTER 10

WHEN DO THE RULES APPLY?

The state championship basketball game was down to the last 8 seconds. The Wildcats were down by two but had possession of the ball. Their coach had called a time out, huddled the team together, and plotted the strategy that he hoped would win the game. Referee whistles blew to resume play. Both teams took their positions on the court. The Wildcats threw the ball to their point guard. All of the sudden, the post player on the wildcats team knelt down on the floor on all fours and began to bark like a dog. The opposing team, the Bulldogs, stopped playing and stared in astonishment. What was wrong with that kid? Their entire team stood still on the court to gawk in amazement. They assumed that play would stop. They were wrong. In the few seconds that it took them to realize what was happening, the Wildcats had scored a basket to win the championship game.

The Bulldogs' coach was furious. He rushed the floor and screamed at the officials. "What's wrong with you? Play should have stopped! That basket shouldn't count." The official retorted, "Sorry coach, I am the official and I never blew the whistle to stop the game. Basket is good."

But this is a book on worship, so how does a basketball game fit into our discussion? Simple. God is the active "Official" in worship. He is the only One Who can say when the rules of worship apply and when they do not. Just because certain people think that the rules of worship should not apply to what they are doing does not make it so. When we approach God in worship, He makes the rules and says when they apply. Let's look at some examples in which people seem to be assuming that God's rules do not apply to what they are doing.

PRAISE TEAMS

It is becoming increasingly popular in denominations and in some churches of Christ to "enhance" the song service. The idea is that a better-led, more energetic song service will help people feel closer to God. To achieve this "enhanced" song service a team of the congregation's "best" singers are assembled. Many times this team is composed of four singers, one for each part of the harmony. Often the singers are two guys, for the bass and tenor and two girls, for the soprano and alto. They often are given microphones and stand on stage. This "praise team" leads the songs, and supposedly everything is "better." But let's think about that for a minute. When we looked at what the Bible says about women's role in public worship, we saw that God does not permit women to lead in the assembly. A praise team that consists of women leading singing is a violation of God's role for women in the assembly. Just because the denominational world around us does it, or we think it sounds better, we cannot throw out God's rules for worship.

In accordance with God's rules, however, two men could stand before a congregation and lead different parts of a song, in order to help the song be sung in an orderly way. There would be no scriptural reason to say that four men could not each sing a different part of a song in order to teach it to a congregation or lead it. The traditional one-song-leader approach is not the **only** scriptural way to do things, although it is **a** Scriptural way to do things. We simply must insist, however, that whatever approach is taken follows God's rules for worship.

CONTEMPORARY CHRISTIAN MUSIC

Another very popular religious innovation is contemporary Christian music. Anything from hard rock "Christian" music to old-time country gospel music can be found in many of the CD and tape players of members of the Church. There are several arguments used to justify listening to contemporary Christian music played with musical instruments. First, some argue that since it is not in a worship assembly, God's rules about singing simply do not apply. Once again, let's think about that. Take, for instance, the song "O, worship the King." What kind of song is that? It is a song of worship to God. Who makes the rules about how we should worship God? God does, of course. Suppose that we sing "O, worship the King" on Sunday morning. What are we doing? We are worshiping God. Now suppose we sing it on Monday morning. What are we doing? We are still worshiping God and His rules still apply. Any time a Christian engages in an avenue of worship, he is bound to follow the biblical guidelines that relate to that act. If the Bible teaches that one should not use an instrument of music in worship, then he should not, on Sunday or Monday or any other day. We cannot deny that an activity is worship just because it takes place on Tuesday morning instead of Sunday morning.

Think about this. The Bible says that in order to pray to God, we should pray in Jesus' name. Now suppose we say that on Sundays in the assembly we should pray to God in Jesus' name, but on Mondays or other days of the week outside of the assembly we can pray through Mary or one of the "saints." Every one of us knows that is not right. When the Bible lays down the guidelines for prayer, those guidelines apply every time we talk to God in prayer. In the same way, when the Bible lays down the guidelines for worshiping God in song without instruments, those guidelines apply all the time.

But many people who argue for contemporary Christian music say, "I think its better to listen to good, wholesome lyrics than the garbage they play on the radio." The problem with this argument is that we are comparing ourselves to others instead of comparing ourselves to what the Bible says. Is it better to watch a movie with 100 curse words in it than to watch one with 500? Is it better to smoke 3 joints at a party or 12? The "it is better" argument does not make anything right. Anybody can think up something that is worse than what they are doing. We must make sure that we apply God's rules of worship whenever we worship.

IT'S NOT REALLY WORSHIP, IT'S ENTERTAINMENT

Many people recognize that proper worship must always be done by God's guidelines. For that reason, some people listen to, or participate in, religious songs with musical instruments, and claim that it is not worship but instead just "entertainment." Therefore, it is argued, the rules for "worship" do not really apply.

The problem with this idea is that simply changing the name from "worship" to "entertainment" does not change the action. If a person is singing "O, worship the King" and not really meaning what he is singing, then that person is worshiping the Lord in vain. Suppose a person said "Oh my God" often without thinking about God, claiming that she is just using the phrase for entertainment. Calling the phrase "entertainment" does not change the fact that God's name is used. When a person uses God's name without thinking about God or uses it for "entertainment," that is using God's name in vain (similar to how the soldiers worshiped Jesus, but who did not really mean it). Any time songs are sung with words of praise and worship in them, then God's rules for worship apply.

MORE ABOUT ENTERTAINMENT

We must remember who our audience is. God is the audience for our worship. Anytime we forget that fact, dangerous practices start to creep in to our worship. For instance, suppose there was a man in a certain congregation who could lead very eloquent prayers. In fact, his prayers were so impressive that certain people in the congregation thought that others should hear just how fine this man's voice sounded when he prayed. So, the man began to travel around to other congregations and lead long, beautiful prayers. He became so well known for his eloquent prayers, that he was invited to hold special prayer services, after the regular services, in which congregations and audiences would sit and listen to him pray, and then clap for him after each prayer, telling him afterward how great he sounded while praying. Would this ever happen? Mostly likely not with prayer. We all have read Jesus' rebuke of the Pharisees. On several occasions, He rebuked them for praying "to be seen by men" (Matthew 6:5). When an act of worship is done to be seen by men, then it is no longer an acceptable act of worship.

We asked if the above scenario would happen with prayer and said probably not. But what if there happened to be a man, or group of people, who were good at singing? Would this man or group sound so good that they would be asked to travel around to different congregations to sing praises in special services while the congregations and the audiences sat silently by and applauded their singing abilities after each song? Would such a group after their "performances" be told how wonderful they sounded and what "meaning" they gave to the songs they sung? Worship is not entertainment and those involved in it should not be performers. We must remember that God is the audience, not men.

Let's take this one step further, however. Could there ever be a case in which it would be appropriate for a man to travel around and pray at different congregations? Sure. Suppose the congregation was composed of new Christians and they needed someone to teach them how to pray. Or suppose that congregation had realized that they had been sinning and they asked this man to come and pray with them and for them. As long as the prayer is a sincere prayer, done according to God's regulations and not "to be seen by men," then the worship is acceptable. In the same way, a person or group of people could have legitimate reasons to travel around singing religious songs. Maybe congregations would like to learn new songs, or maybe they would like to learn a new way to sing old songs. We must be sure, however, that the reasons are valid and not simply because the people who are singing sound good to us. Any legitimate act of worship that is done for the **purpose** of gaining the approval of men **looses** its value and becomes **useless** worship, which was Jesus point in Mathew 6:1-17.

CONCLUSION

The list of "what ifs" could go on for a mile. What about drama teams? What about small groups? What about vocal noises that sound like musical instruments? What about....? We cannot give you all the answers for such things, because we simply do not know all the answers. We do know, however, that every act of worship must conform to the rules that God has established. God's regulations for singing and praying are the same on Mondays as they are on Sundays. No person or group should ever put women in a teaching or leading role in the public assembly. Worship should never be used as entertainment, and individuals or groups should never attempt to "sound good" just to be seen by men. Let's make sure that the first question we ask when considering any of these matters is: What has God requested?

DISCUSSION QUESTIONS

1. What do you think is the number one reason many people disregard certain rules in situations like certain worship practices? Give one reason offered in the chapter. What validity does the "everybody's doing it" argument have? (Uses verses like Proverbs 1:10,15 and 1 Corinthians 15:33 in your answer)

2. Is there any type of "praise team" that could be scriptural? Explain your answer. What kinds of "praise teams" are not according to Scripture? Explain your answer.

3. What are several different avenues of worship? Who designed these avenues of worship? How has God asked us to worship Him through music? How has God instructed us to pray? When do the rules for proper worship through music or prayer apply?

4. Explain the "I think it's better" argument. What is the crucial flaw in this argument? Show the flaw by listing several examples.

5. What are several problems with the idea of using worship as entertainment? How does Matthew 6:1-7 apply to the discussion? List and discuss other "what if" situations and work through how the rules for worship apply to them.

"But the fruit of the Spirit is love, joy, peace, longsuffering, kindness, goodness, faithfulness, gentleness, self-control."

Galatians 5:22-23

We should be thankful and excited about the Spirit's work. At the same time we should refuse to listen to teachers who claim the Holy Spirit is working in ways the Bible does not teach.

CHAPTER 11

THE HOLY SPIRIT

Jill had never been to church before. Her family did not go anywhere; so when her friend Amy Sullivan asked her to spend the night on Saturday and then go to church with her on Sunday, Jill was nervous and excited at the same time. She had heard about Jesus from some of her friends. She even knew the words to "Jesus Loves Me," although she couldn't remember where she'd learned them. But lately she'd been thinking a lot about life and death, right and wrong, and she thought going to church might be just what she needed.

As the Sullivans pulled into the parking lot on Sunday morning, Jill could barely contain her nervous excitement. The church sign in the parking lot had moveable black letters that spelled "Holy Spirit—Catch the Fire Here." There were already lots of people there, even though the Sullivans were twenty minutes early. A huge banner over the door said, "Welcome Holy Spirit." Already, many questions were going through Jill's mind.

As she sat down next to Amy in a long row of cushioned chairs she looked around the large room that Amy had called "the sanctuary." There were probably 200 chairs lined up in neat rows with a ten-foot walkway down the middle. At the front of the room there was a large open space in front of a stage. What caught Jill's eye on stage were the instruments. There was a HUGE set of drums, three guitars, two keyboards stacked on top of one another; smaller instruments like tambourines and maracas were piled in a box next to one of four microphones—enough instruments and sound equipment to make most mediocre local rock bands extremely jealous. The surface of the big bass drum identified the band as "Soul Watch." There was also a transparent podium on stage. Jill guessed that's where the preacher must stand to preach. But it was pretty obvious that the big attraction here was the music and the Holy Spirit, whatever that was. Between the Holy Spirit and this band, Jill was sure this was going to be very exciting.

Over the course of the next two hours Jill witnessed all kinds of things that were new to her. "This is wild," she kept thinking to herself. The rock band was great. The drums were loud, and the guitar player was awesome. The audience raised their hands in the air and swayed from side to side just like at a rock concert. Occasionally someone would shout "Hallelujah" or "Praise the Lord." Sometimes members of the audience would clap along, or dance in the aisles or the open space up front. Jill didn't catch many of the words to the songs, but she had a vague impression that most of them were about Jesus. After the music, there was a "healing service" where sick people went forward to be healed. A woman up front prayed loudly to God, Jesus, and the Holy Spirit and put her hands on the sick people. They went away smiling and crying, saying "Thank you Jesus" and "Hallelujah." Jill couldn't tell if they were really healed, but they sure acted like they felt better.

Finally when it came time for the preacher to talk, he stood up with his Bible and said, "I didn't study or plan anything to say today, but I know that the Spirit will tell me all He wants us to know." He then preached for an hour, constantly reminding the people that the real source of this lesson was the Holy Spirit. At some points in the service, people would yell out or shake. Two women even passed out. At the end of the lesson three people came forward who had received "Holy Spirit Baptism" during the sermon. These three people spoke garbled words which nobody in the room could understand. (Amy later explained that they were "speaking in tongues, like in the Bible.") After the last "Hallelujah," the audience streamed out of "the sanctuary" to their cars. Jill heard several people say that "the Holy Spirit sure was on us today." Jill had some strange feelings that she couldn't explain, and she wondered if that was the Holy Spirit working on her. She decided that it probably was, and then she went to eat lunch at Shoney's with the Sullivans.

The story about Jill and her first "church experience" describes several mistaken beliefs that many people have about the Holy Spirit.

Conversations about the Holy Spirit make many Christians nervous. He's powerful and confusing. He works in us, but we're not exactly sure how. There's so much false teaching and misunderstanding about the Holy Spirit that most Christians find it easier not to deal with the subject at all. So we haven't dealt with it. We haven't talked about it, and more importantly, we haven't studied it. False teaching about the Holy Spirit is sneaking its way into the Church, and we find ourselves incapable, not only of fighting the false teaching, but also of defining our own beliefs about the Holy Spirit.

The Holy Spirit is a big topic. It is like saying, "Today we'll be learning about Jesus." The Holy Spirit is a topic just as huge. The Holy Spirit is one of the three persons that make up God. The Holy Spirit as God was present at the creation of the world (Genesis 1:2). Jesus said that sinners were to be baptized "in the name of the Father and of the Son and of the Holy Spirit" (Matthew 28: 18). The Holy Spirit is a member of the God-head, and to attempt to fully understand Him in a few short pages would be impossible. So we'll have to be content with looking at a few things the Holy Spirit does not do today and a few things that He does.

A FEW THINGS THE HOLY SPIRIT DOES NOT DO TODAY

The Holy Spirit does not enable people today to work miracles or speak in tongues.

We do need to know that the Holy Spirit did things in the New Testament that He is not doing today. The apostles and early Christians on whom the apostles laid their hands were able to do miraculous things. They could heal, prophesy, and speak in actual languages they had not studied, in addition to being able to work other miracles. They could even be bitten by poisonous snakes without getting hurt. But these miracles were limited to the time of the apostles because of the plan of God. The apostles could pass on the ability to work miracles, but others could not (Acts 8:18). So when the apostles died there was no way to pass on these miraculous powers.

In fact, the New Testament taught that the miraculous powers of the Holy Spirit were only temporary. The Holy Spirit, through Paul, in 1 Corinthians 13:8 said: "Love never fails. But whether there are prophecies, they will fail; whether there are tongues, they will cease; whether there is knowledge, it will vanish away." Every Christian has the gift of the Holy Spirit (Acts 2:38), but NO Christian today has the miraculous gifts of the Holy Spirit. What, then, does the gift of the Holy Spirit do for a Christian, if is not power to do miracles? Galatians 5:22-23 tells us that the "fruit of the Spirit is love, joy, peace, longsuffering, kindness, goodness, faithfulness, gentleness, self-control." The Holy Spirit helps us to have these qualities today, but He no longer gives Christians the ability to do miracles, as He once did in the first century.

The Holy Spirit does not cause chaos and confusion.

During Jill's first church experience she kept thinking, "This is wild." The scene was chaotic, disorganized, and confusing. People were dancing, falling on the floor, and babbling incoherently. This is not how the Holy Spirit works. "God is not the author of confusion..." (1 Corinthians 14:33). He wants all things to be "done decently and in order" (verse 40). The wild, uninhibited "concert feel" is not an atmosphere created by the Holy Spirit. It is an atmosphere created by loud music, wild imaginations, and emotionalism.

The Holy Spirit does not give words to those who have not studied or prepared.

All of the words of the Bible are the product of the Holy Spirit (2 Peter 1:21), but the Holy Spirit will not miraculously or spontaneously put them in our mouths. Timothy, a young preacher, had received a special gift (probably the ability to do miracles), but he was still commanded to be "diligent to present yourself approved to God, a worker who does not need to be ashamed, rightly dividing the word of truth" (2 Timothy 2:15). The Holy Spirit directed the apostles in what they should say when they stood before kings and governors to defend their cause (read Matthew 10:17-21). But that was only for the apostles. In fact, the apostles instructed their listeners to read and study the Word. Peter said be "ready to give a defense to everyone who asks you a reason for the hope that is in you" (1 Peter 3:15). The ability to teach and explain the Word of God takes study, preparation, and prayer—not a miracle from the Holy Spirit.

A FEW THINGS THE HOLY SPIRIT DOES TODAY

The Holy Spirit teaches us the will of God through the Word of God.

The Bible is the work of the Holy Spirit. The Holy Spirit moved men to write down for us the will of God. Peter explained that the Word of God is for all men, sent from the Holy Spirit: "knowing this first, that no prophecy of Scripture is of any private interpretation, for prophecy never came by the will of man, but holy men of God spoke as they were moved by the Holy Spirit" (2 Peter 1:20-21). The words of the Bible are God's own words for us. To say that the Bible is "inspired" by God or the Holy Spirit means, literally, that it is "God-breathed." Paul told Timothy, "All Scripture is given by inspiration of God, and is profitable for doctrine, for reproof, for correction, for instruction in righteousness, that the man of God may be complete, thoroughly equipped for every good work" (2 Timothy 3:16-17). The Holy Spirit has given us words that should direct our lives. They are the words of the Bible. We cannot learn them spontaneously and miraculously, but only by learning the Scriptures and applying them to our actions.

The Holy Spirit works in cooperation with our spirits.

The Holy Spirit will never guide us somewhere we are not willing to go. He will never overrule our free will or freedom of choice. He will not make us do right; nor will He prevent us from doing wrong. Romans 8:16 says, "The Spirit Himself bears witness with our spirit that we are children of God." The Holy Spirit guides us through His inspired Word, the Bible. He works along side our willing spirits to help us and to aid us—"the Spirit also helps in our weaknesses" (Romans 8:26). But He only does this as we choose. When we live lives of sin, we choose to reject the Spirit and the life He wants for us (Romans 8:1-11). But the life led by the teachings of the Spirit and dedicated to cooperation with the Spirit, will produce godly results—what the Bible calls "the fruit of the Spirit." According to Galatians 5:22-23, this "fruit of the Spirit is love, joy, peace, longsuffering, kindness, goodness, faithfulness, gentleness, self-control...." The Christian who follows the teachings of the Holy Spirit—the Bible—and consciously works to apply these teachings to his life will produce this "fruit of the Spirit."

The Holy Spirit helps in our prayers.

Have you ever been in a situation where you just did not know what to pray for? There seemed to be no good thing to ask for or no apparent way out of trouble. You went to the Lord in prayer, but you just didn't know what to say. The Bible says the Holy Spirit helps in times just like that. Romans 8:26-27 says, "For we do not know what we should pray for as we ought, but the Spirit Himself makes intercession for us with groanings which cannot be uttered. Now He who searches the hearts knows what the mind of the Spirit is, because He makes intercession for the saints according to the will of God." Because God, in the form of the Holy Spirit, works in cooperation with our human spirits, He knows us better than we know ourselves. Because of His complete knowledge and His complete power, He is able to help us in prayer, determining what it is we need most when we ourselves are too confused to know.

CONCLUSION

There are certainly many more things that we could investigate—the things the Spirit does today and things He does not do today. But let's just notice a few words in closing. The work of the Holy Spirit is not loud, confusing, sensational, or miraculous today. The Holy Spirit works on behalf of Christians through their willing lives and fervent prayers. We should be thankful and excited about the Spirit's work. At the same time we should refuse to listen to teachers who claim the Holy Spirit is working in ways the Bible does not teach. The study of the Holy Spirit is fascinating and encouraging. It is also the work of a lifetime. We can know about the Holy Spirit but only as we open God's Word to learn about Him.

DISCUSSION QUESTIONS

1. Who is Holy Spirit? How does the Holy Spirit relate to the Father and the Son? Where was the Holy Spirit during the creation of the Universe? In what names are sinners supposed to be baptized?

2. Does the Holy Spirit help people perform miracles today? Explain your answer. Was there ever a time when the Holy Spirit helped people do miracles? Why was this the case? Give Bible verses that would verify your answer.

3. What relationship does the Holy Spirit have with assemblies where there is much confusion and "wild" behavior? Read 1 Corinthians 14:31-32. Even if the Holy Spirit still helped people speak in tongues, how should an assembly with tongue-speakers behave? Will the Holy Spirit ever "take over" a person and make them say or do things they do not decide to do? (Read 1 Corinthians 14 for help with the answer.)

4. Does the Holy Spirit "inspire" sermons in people today? List some Bible verses to prove your answer. When people claim that the Holy Spirit "tells" them what to preach, and they make minor (or major) mistakes in quoting Scripture or other facts, what does that prove? If the Holy Spirit did still inspire people's sermons, how would those sermons relate to Scripture?

5. List and discuss at least three things that the Holy Spirit does. Give Bible verses to validate your answer. What happens with the Holy Spirit when a person is baptized and becomes a Christian? (Read 1 John 3:24 and Acts 2:38 for help with your answer).

"And do not be conformed to this world, but be transformed by the renewing of your mind, that you may prove what is that good and acceptable and perfect will of God."

Romans 12:2

Is there a right way to decide if something is right or wrong? To answer that question, we must ask ourselves what makes something wrong or right?

CHAPTER 12

RIGHT AND WRONG

Is it right to have sex with your boyfriend or girlfriend? Ask that question to 20 different students and teachers at your school, and you will probably get 19 different answers. One girl would probably explain that it is alright, as long as you have been dating at least three months and as long as you "really love each other." At least one teacher would probably say that it is not wise, "Because young people this age are not mature enough to handle the emotional consequences." Ask certain students and they might say it is fine, even if you don't "love each other; after all, it's just sex." Other students might say that it is wrong because their parents say so. You might even have someone say that it is wrong because the Bible says it is wrong.

If you decide to research the question and go to the "experts" you will get just as many different answers. Some "experts" say it is "natural," others say high school students are too young and should wait until they mature. Some experts believe high schoolers should be given an unlimited supply of condoms and free reign to experiment with as many partners as they wish. With so many different answers, how can you choose the correct one? Who has the right to decide if it is right or wrong to have sex before you are married?

MORALITY

We have entered the study of morality. Morality is a word used for the way people determine what is right and what is wrong. When a person makes a moral decision, that person is trying to determine which way is right and which is wrong. How can a person decide? Many people have different ways of doing this. Some think that if it feels good, then it is right and should be done. Others believe they should do the things they think will help the most people. Still others think that the right thing to do is the thing that feels right at the time. How do you personally decide what is right?

Is there a right way to decide if something is right or wrong? To answer that question, we must ask ourselves what makes something wrong or right? Suppose you go into a gas station and steal a pack of crackers and give them to a homeless man on the street. Have you done wrong? Most of us would say that you have done wrong. Why? You just fed a homeless man. Is the action wrong because you stole something? But you were stealing from the "rich" and giving to the poor, just like Robin Hood. Why is it wrong to steal?

A HIGHER LAW

A quick look at the Nazi party in Germany will help us decide. The leading men and generals in Germany killed millions of Jews, blacks, poles, and gypsies. After they lost the war, the Allied Powers put the leading Nazi leaders on trial for their war crimes. The Nazi generals said that they had done nothing wrong. According to them, it was not against their laws to kill Jews. In fact, the laws of Germany at that time said it was good and right. Therefore, they claimed, if German laws allowed it, then it was alright for them to do such things. This defense, however, did not work. They were convicted based on the fact that they had broken certain laws. The laws they broke were not regional, meaning that they were not just for a certain part of the world. They were convicted because they had broken "higher laws" that are for everyone at all times.

We all understand that murdering six million Jews breaks some type of "higher law," but whose law is it? The simple answer to that is "God's Law." If there were no God, then there would be no "higher laws." Every person or society could do whatever they wanted to do, whenever they wanted to do it. But God is the Lawgiver Who has made "higher laws," for all nations and for all times. It might be acceptable to drive 100 miles an hour in Europe on the Autobahn, because the law says it is alright. But it is never okay to murder millions of Jews, even if your government says it is.

Take the issue of abortion for instance. The United States government has made it legal to kill unborn children. Just because it is legal, does that make it right? Absolutely not! The Bible says that God hates the hands that shed innocent blood (Proverbs 6:17). Nothing is more innocent than an unborn child. The leaders who make such rules and the citizens who use them to kill their children will all have to answer to the ultimate Lawgiver, who has not given anyone the authority to murder innocent children.

There we have it. Once again, the question of morality (just like authority) goes back to God. To put it simply: what God says is right, is right; what He says is wrong, is wrong. He created humans and He knows exactly how we should behave in order to live happy, healthy, productive lives. He also knows that sinful, destructive behavior is harmful to our well being. The moral principles and laws He has made are in place to encourage us to do right so that we will be happy.

GOD SPEAKS ABOUT HOMOSEXUALITY

Let's apply God's morality to a few areas of life that some people are wondering about today. Let's start with homosexuality. On most television channels and in most movies, Hollywood makes sure to have a homosexual character. Most of the time, this character is "cool." He is handsome and funny, and all the girls love talking to him. When it is a girl, she is pretty and charming, and she gets along with the guys well. These homosexual characters laugh and tell jokes, and are portrayed as happy as (or happier than) the others. They simply live an "alternate lifestyle." This lifestyle is pushed as something that is right and good. And, although it might not be for everyone, we should all at least accept that some people are "that way" and not "condemn" them for their choice. In fact, in the news, you have probably seen homosexual couples getting married in certain states, having wedding ceremonies, and adopting children. Is this lifestyle acceptable? Can people who are homosexuals help the way they are?

To answer these questions, we must go to the Bible (remember that only God has the right to make the rules when it comes to right and wrong). The Bible often talks about homosexuality. In each case, it describes the practice as sin. Paul, in the first chapter of Romans, gave a long list of sins. In that list, he wrote about homosexuality when he said:

> "For this reason God gave them up to vile passions. For even their women exchanged the natural use for what is against nature. Likewise also the men, leaving the natural use of the woman, burned in their lust for one another, men with men committing what is shameful, and receiving in themselves the penalty of their error which was due" (Romans 1:26-27).

Again, in 1 Corinthians 6:9-11, the Bible says:

> "Do you not know that the unrighteous will not inherit the kingdom of God? Do not be deceived. Neither fornicators, nor idolaters, nor adulterers, nor homosexuals, nor sodomites, nor thieves, nor covetous, nor drunkards, nor revilers, nor extortioners will inherit the kingdom of God. And such were some of you. But you were washed, but you were sanctified, but you were justified in the name of the Lord Jesus and by the Spirit of our God."

In both verses it is clear that God views homosexuality as a sin. In fact, he says that those who practice this sin without repenting "will not inherit the kingdom of God." It is a sin because God made sex a wonderful activity to be experienced only in a proper marriage between a husband and a wife (read Matthew 19:1-10). God says sex is for marriage, and marriage is only for a man and a woman. Homosexuality goes against God's original pattern.

The Bible tells us that some of the Corinthians were homosexuals before they became Christians. When they repented, stopped their sinful practice, and became Christians they were washed and forgiven of their sins (1 Corinthians 6:11). Homosexuality is a sin. God loves homosexual people, but He hates the sin of homosexuality. If homosexuals do not change their sinful lifestyle, they will not inherit the kingdom of God.

While we are discussing sexuality, let's go back to our first question: Is it right to have sex with your boyfriend or girlfriend? Refer back to our discussion about homosexuality. God created sex as a wonderful, fun, exciting activity within a proper marriage. If you are not married to your boyfriend or girlfriend, then it is wrong to have sex with him or her. The same passage that talks about homosexuals not inheriting the kingdom of God also mentions that "fornicators" are in the same boat. What are "fornicators?" People who have sex before they are married are fornicators. Fornication is just as sinful as homosexuality. Anyone who continues to practice such things without repenting will not go to heaven.

HOW FAR IS TOO FAR

But what about other things that are not technically sex—things like touching underneath clothing or romantic caressing? How far can a boyfriend and girlfriend go? In the Bible, you have probably run across a couple of twenty-dollar words that you did not completely understand: licentiousness and lasciviousness (read 1 Peter 4:3). These words basically apply to things that might not technically be sex, but are still wrong. Things like dirty dancing and caressing certain parts of the body would be included in these terms. In fact, the question: "How far is too far?" is actually the wrong question to ask. Since the Bible says that the body of the Christian belongs to the Lord (1 Corinthians 6:12-18), we should be asking, "Will this bring glory to God?," or "Will this help me be a better Christian?" If we remember that God is always there with us, we will be much less likely to try to push the limits. Is what you are doing with your boyfriend or girlfriend something you would do if Jesus were sitting in the car with you? Now that is a good question.

PORNOGRAPHY

While we are talking frankly about sex and things like it, we need to spend a little time on pornography. This generation has easier access to more filthy, pornographic material than any previous generation. In fact, if you are like most teens, a large percentage of you who are reading this book have gone to Websites, movies, or magazines and looked at porno pictures at least a time or two. Is looking at pornography wrong? Once again, we must determine what the Bible says.

In Matthew 5:27-28, Jesus Christ said: "You have heard that it was said to those of old, 'You shall not commit adultery.' But I say to you that whoever looks at a woman to lust for her has already committed adultery with her in his heart." In these verses, Jesus showed us that sin can be in the mind. A person never has to touch another person to commit lust. Simply thinking about another person in a sexual situation, like lusting after them on a Website for example, would be sin. The apostle Paul said, "Finally, brethren, whatever things are true, whatever things are noble, whatever things are just, whatever things are pure, whatever things are lovely, whatever things are of good report, if there is any virtue and if there is anything praiseworthy—meditate on these things" (Philippians 4:8). Pornography certainly would not fit into any of these wholesome categories. It is addictive and dangerous. If you have been looking at pornography, stop, and find some way to keep yourself away from it. Satan has used pornography to destroy the minds and souls of millions of people.

CONCLUSION

The list of moral decisions could go on and on. Is it right to drink alcohol? What about smoking? Is it a sin to smoke marijuana? Is it wrong to go to parties where there will be lots of drinking? Is it a sin to go to places where dirty dancing is taking place? Is it a sin to wear a bikini on the beach?

If we remember and practice one single principle, many of these decisions will be made for us. We must remember that the body of the Christian belongs to the Lord. Romans 12:1-2 explains that the body of the Christian should be given to the Lord as a living sacrifice that brings glory to God. That means we should avoid things that would intentionally harm our bodies. (Getting drunk is a good example of something that harms the body, read Proverbs 23:29-35.) And we should not put ourselves in situations where we would not want to be found when the Lord comes again. How far is too far? Should I drink this? Should I wear this? Most all of these questions really boil down to the question, "Would God be proud of this decision?" The truth is, most of us **know** what is right, **doing** what we know is right is our biggest challenge.

DISCUSSION QUESTIONS

1. What is morality? Why do you think there are so many different opinions concerning which things are right and which things are wrong?

2. How should a person determine which things are right and wrong? How does a study of the Nazi party in Germany fit into this discussion?

3. What does the Bible teach about abortion? What does the Bible teach about homosexuality? If the government makes things like abortion or homosexual marriage legal, does that change how they should be viewed morally?

4. What does the Bible teach about premarital sex? Do you think many of the people who have premarital sex know what the Bible says about it? If so, why do you think so many people continue to engage in this sin?

5. What makes God the perfect Being to decide what is right and what is wrong? What would happen if morality was determined by a majority vote? What are some wrong ways that people attempt to make moral decisions?

"But the day of the Lord will come as a thief in the night, in which the heavens will pass away with a great noise, and the elements will melt with fervent heat; both the earth and the works that are in it will be burned up."

2 Peter 3:10

There will be no physical reign on Earth. When Christ comes back, the physical Universe will melt and dissolve.

CHAPTER 13

WHEN JESUS COMES AGAIN

The scene was crazy. Cars with bumper stickers that read, "In Case of Rapture, this car will be driverless," had suddenly veered off the road, smashing into curbs, trees, telephone poles, and ditches. Entire bus loads of people looked up to see their drivers missing. Brain surgeons, in the middle of surgery, vanished into thin air, leaving their patients unconscious on the surgery table. Air traffic control operators disappeared, leaving the in-flight planes in hopeless confusion. Not to mention the fact that several pilots had vanished while flying, sending their planes crashing to the ground. "It's the Rapture!" cried one frantic lady in the middle of New York City. Cries of "The Rapture!, The Rapture!" echoed through every city and street. Reporters rushed from church building to church building asking church leaders what was going on. "It's the Rapture," commented one denominational leader. "I should have been ready, but I wasn't. But He'll be coming back in a few years to set up His earthly Kingdom and reign for a thousand years. I'll be ready then." "Where are you getting this information?" asked the reporter. "It's in the Bible. That's what it says will happen," replied the religious man.

Hold that thought. If you have seen any of the *Left Behind* books or movies, you are quite familiar with this idea of the Rapture and a thousand year reign of Christ on the Earth. In fact, you have probably heard of the huge battle called Armageddon that many religious people think will take place at the end of the world. According to this idea, when Jesus came to set up His earthly kingdom in the first century, He was unexpectedly rejected by the Jewish nation. His plans to set up an earthly kingdom were messed up at that time and He was crucified. After coming back from the dead, He supposedly promised to come back to this Earth and set up the kingdom that did not get established the first time He tried. Millions of religious people, denominations, and even some members of the Church of Christ are beginning to teach that seven years before He comes to set up this earthly kingdom there will be a rapture. In this rapture, all of the faithful people supposedly will be zapped out of their normal lives in an instant, leaving their buses running, planes flying, patients waiting, and the like.

Where do these people get this idea? They claim to get it from the Bible, but the Bible does not teach that Christ's mission in the first century was incomplete. And it does not teach that His rejection by the Jews was unexpected. Nor does it teach that Christ will ever come back to this Earth to set up a physical kingdom. In fact, the Bible teaches the exact opposite. The Bible says that Christ's mission was completed exactly as He planned in the first century. It also teaches that when Christ returns, the Earth and all the physical matter in the Universe will be destroyed. In this chapter we are going to learn what the Bible really says about Christ's Second Coming, and why many have been misled about it.

CHRIST DID WHAT HE CAME TO DO

When the apostle Peter stood up on the day of Pentecost to preach the good news of Christ in Acts 2, he used several Old Testament prophecies to prove that Jesus is the Messiah sent from God. In those Old Testament verses, Peter explained that the suffering of Christ, His death, and His resurrection were all planned by God. In Acts 2:23 Peter said, "Him [Jesus], being delivered by **the determined counsel and foreknowledge of God**, you have taken by lawless hands, have crucified, and put to death...." Just a few short verses later, Peter talked about a prophecy made by David almost 1,000 years before Jesus came to the Earth. Peter explained that David was a prophet and that he foresaw that Christ would rise from the dead (Acts 2:31). Christ's death on the cross instigated by the Jews was not an unexpected event. Instead, it happened exactly as He planned it. Christ does not need to come back to this Earth to finish something that He "didn't quite get done" when He was here the first time. He established His Church, which is the Kingdom of God on this Earth (Matthew 16:13-20), exactly as the Old Testament predicted.

EVERYTHING PHYSICAL AND MATERIAL WILL BURN

In very straightforward language, the Bible explains that when Christ comes back a second time, all matter in the Universe will be destroyed. Second Peter 3:10-13 says:

"But the day of the Lord will come as a thief in the night, in which the heavens will pass away with a great noise, and the elements will melt with fervent heat; both the earth and the works that are in it will be burned up. Therefore, since all these things will be dissolved, what manner of persons ought you to be in holy conduct and godliness, looking for and hastening the coming of the day of God, because of which the heavens will be dissolved, being on fire, and the elements will melt with fervent heat? Nevertheless we, according to His promise, look for new heavens and a new earth in which righteousness dwells."

These verses clearly state that when Jesus comes again, everything material—"heavens, elements, the earth, and all the works that are in it"—will be burned up or dissolved. All the elements will "melt with fervent heat." The new heavens and new earth mentioned in the verse will not be a "remake" of the old. They will be a spiritual realm where souls can live, not made of physical matter like the Universe is now.

WHAT WILL HAPPEN TO THE FAITHFUL?

We read that all matter, elements, heavens, and Earth will be burned, dissolved, and melted. But what will happen to the people who are living on the Earth (and who have died) when the Lord comes again? In the first century, many Christians asked this same question. In fact, some of the early Christians thought that they needed to be alive when Christ comes back in order to get the "full benefits." In 1 Thessalonians 4:13-18, Paul answered their questions and put their fears to rest:

> But I do not want you to be ignorant brethren, concerning those who have fallen asleep [died], lest you sorrow as others who have no hope. For if we believe that Jesus died and rose again, even so God will bring with Him those who sleep in Jesus. For this we say to you by the word of the Lord, that we who are alive and remain until the coming of the Lord will by no means precede those who are asleep. For the Lord Himself will descend from heaven with a shout, with the voice of an archangel, and with the trumpet of God. And the dead in Christ will rise first. Then we who are alive and remain shall be caught up together with them in the clouds to meet the Lord in the air. And thus we shall always be with the Lord. Therefore comfort one another with these words.

From these verses, we can see that those faithful to the Lord who die before the Lord returns and all the faithful who are alive when He comes back will meet Jesus together in the air, not on the Earth. But what about their bodies? Will the faithful meet Jesus in their physical bodies? If all the physical things of this Earth are going to be destroyed, what will happen to our physical bodies? It is funny you should ask, because the early Christians had a very similar question. Paul once again gives us the answer. In 1 Corinthians 15:50-53, he said:

> Now this I say, brethren, that flesh and blood cannot inherit the kingdom of God; nor does corruption inherit incorruption. Behold, I tell you a mystery: We shall not all sleep, but we shall be changed—in a moment, in the twinkling of an eye, at the last trumpet. For the trumpet will sound, and the dead will be raised incorruptible, and we shall all be changed. For this corruptible must put on incorruption, and this mortal must put on immortality.

There is our answer. All those faithful followers of God who die before Christ comes again will be raised with a new, incorruptible spiritual body. All those who are alive will be changed in "a twinkling of an eye" and be given a new, spiritual body (1 Corinthians 15:44,52). There will be no physical reign on Earth. When Christ comes back, the physical Universe will melt and dissolve.

THE BOOK OF REVELATION

After looking at several passages of Scripture, we can see what is going to happen when Jesus comes again. But where do the ideas about the rapture, a 1,000 year reign, and Armageddon come from? Many of these ideas are taken from misunderstandings about the book of Revelation.

If you have read the book of Revelation, then you know that it is a very "interesting" book. It discusses angels pouring out bowls of wrath on the Earth, wicked angels that are thrown into deep pits, dragons, women who are given wings to fly, and a host of other things you might find in fairy tales or fictional writing. What do all those things mean? And how can we understand them?

Signs, Signs, Everywhere Signs

One of the most important things to remember about the book of Revelation is that it is a book of signs. The first verse of the book says, "The Revelation of Jesus Christ, which God gave Him to show His servants—things which must shortly take place. And He sent and **signified** it by His angel to His servant John."

That word "signified" means that Jesus used "signs" to get His message to John. When we think of "signs," many of us think about things that are supposed to happen just before an event, or that point to an event. But that is not exactly what this first verse of Revelation means. Most all of the "signs" in Revelation are symbols that stand for something else, and are not supposed to be taken literally. Let's see how that works.

In Revelation 1, the apostle John saw seven golden lamp stands, and he saw "One like the Son of Man" in the middle of the lamp stands. This person "had in His right hand seven stars," and "out of His mouth went a sharp two-edged sword" (Revelation 1:16). Wow! A man in the middle of seven lamp stands with seven stars in His right hand and a sharp sword coming out of His mouth! What does all that mean? Remember that we said the book of Revelation uses symbols that are not meant to be literal. These things are symbols that stand for something else. When we read further in chapter one, the Bible explains that the seven lamp stands represent the seven churches of Asia, and the seven stars stand for the messengers of those churches (1:20). But what does the sharp sword in the man's mouth mean? In Ephesians 6:17, Paul tells the Christians to "take the helmet of salvation, **and the sword of the Spirit, which is the word of God**." In Hebrews 4:12, we read that the "**the word of God is living and powerful, and sharper than any two-edged sword.**" The picture, then, in Revelation chapter one that at first seemed very strange now makes sense. Jesus (the One like the Son of Man) is in the middle of the seven churches in Asia (the seven golden lamp stands), using the Word of God (the sharp sword in His mouth) to judge them and set them straight. All those signs make perfect sense when you know what they stand for.

It is interesting to think that we use signs or metaphors similar to this every day. For instance, suppose someone told you that his dog "kicked the bucket." If you were not familiar with the phrase "kicked the bucket" you might think that your friend had a ninja dog that could really kick buckets. If you know what the phrase means, however, you know that your friend's dog died. Now suppose your friend wrote that phrase in a letter that was found 2,000 years later, in a time when the phrase was no longer used. Would the readers have a hard time understanding the symbolism? Yes.

That is why the book of Revelation is sometimes difficult to understand. It is a book of apocalyptic language. This apocalyptic language was much more easily understood by the Christians. In apocalyptic language, horns often stood for kings, beasts were symbols for nations, and many other symbols were used and recognized (the books of Ezekiel and Daniel also contain this type of language). These symbols were not to be taken literally. What if you said that in college football this week the elephants rolled over the tigers in Alabama. For those of us who know the mascots of college football teams, we know that the elephants represent the University of Alabama and the tigers stand for Auburn. Suppose we were talking politics and we said the elephants routed the donkeys in last year's election. In economics, we might say that we are in the middle of a bull market, after last year's bear market. We understand that these symbols stand for something else.

Armageddon and the 1,000 Year Reign

With that in mind, let's go back to Revelation. In chapter 19, we read about a huge battle that takes place in which Jesus sits on a white horse and fights against "the beast, the 'false prophet,' and all who had 'the mark of the beast.'" Christ captured these, and the rest who fought against Him "were killed with the sword which proceeded from the mouth of Him who sat on the horse." Looking at this scene, remembering the symbolism involved, we can see that Christ is fighting against the forces of evil using "the sword," to judge the evildoers (which is the Word of God, read John 12:42). This is not a physical battle, but a spiritual battle between the forces of good and evil. Just like Paul said that Christians are currently fighting the forces of spiritual evil (Ephesians 6: 12). This scene in Revelation is not going to be a literal battle scene that takes place on the Earth, it is a spiritual battle scene in which the Word of God is used to fight all those who do not obey it.

In the next chapter of Revelation, we read about an angel grabbing a dragon, and binding him with a chain for 1,000 years. We are told the dragon is the symbol for the devil. But it is here that many stop looking at the symbols, and say that the 1,000 years is a literal period of time when Christ will reign on the Earth. We cannot, however, look at the symbols throughout the entire book of Revelation, and then dismiss them when it fits with a certain teaching that we like. The dragon is a symbol for the devil, the chain is a symbol for God restraining the devil, and the 1,000 years is not a literal period of time, but stands for a long period of time. The 1,000-reign is symbolic just like the other symbols in the nearby verses, and in the rest of the book.

CONCLUSION

The Bible gives us a clear picture of what will take place when Christ comes back a second time. Everything physical will be burned, melted, and dissolved, and all the faithful men and women will be changed (glorified) in the twinkling of an eye into spiritual beings who will live with Christ forever. There will be no physical battle on the Earth and no literal thousand year reign. Furthermore, certain people will not be zapped out of their places seven years before the final coming of Christ. Instead, "the Lord Himself will descend from heaven with a shout, with the voice of an archangel, and with the trumpet of God. And the dead in Christ will rise first. Then we who are alive and remain shall be caught up together with them in the clouds to meet the Lord in the air. And thus we shall always be with the Lord. Therefore comfort one another with these words" (1 Thessalonians 4:16-18).

DISCUSSION QUESTIONS

1. What is the modern idea called the Rapture? Discuss what many people think will happen at the end of the world. Before reading this chapter, what did you think was going to happen at the Second Coming of Jesus?

2. Did Jesus get caught off guard when the Jewish leaders crucified Him? How do you know? What did Jesus come to do the first time He came? Did He get done what He wanted to get done?

3. When Jesus comes again, what will happen to this physical Universe (read 2 Peter 3:10-13)? When this happens, what will happen to the Christians who are alive? What will happen to the ones who die before Christ comes again?

4. In the book of Revelation, what does the word "signify" in 1:1 mean? Discuss some of the symbols found in chapter one like the lampstands, the sword, and the stars. What do these symbols "signify"?

5. Discuss several modern "symbols" or signs that we would understand but people several years from now probably would not. What kind of literature is the Book of Revelation? (Hint: several Old Testament books have this same kind of writing in them.) In this kind of literature, what do horns often stand for? What about beasts? How should the 1,000 year reign and Armageddon be understood? Why?

AFTERWORD

Well that's it. That's the end...of this book anyway.

We know that there are many more questions that you might have on many more issues. There is really only one book that can answer all our questions about what God wants from us, and we probably don't have to tell you which book that is. Although we will any way—the Bible. And it's the ruler by which we must measure every practice in the Lord's Church. Satan will continue to tempt us to "hop on the bandwagon," put down our defenses, and join the religious crowd in doing things that God does not permit. We must not be tricked by teachers and leaders from in our churches or from outside who would pressure us to give up our special identity as the Church that belongs to Christ.

Your generation is currently in the process of becoming the leaders of the Lord's Church. You will face hard decisions about the worship, practices, and doctrines of the Church. The good news is that all the answers are in one place. Jesus taught "everyone who hears these sayings of mine and does them, I will liken him to a wise man who built his house on the rock." Your faith, built on the rock-solid foundation of God's Word, will not be destroyed by storms of trouble ...or waves of change.